Teaching the
Selected Works of
Mildred D. Taylor

The Young Adult Novels in the Classroom Series

When former Heinemann–Boynton/Cook editor Peter Stillman first conceived the Young Adult Literature (YAL) series in 1990 and asked me to be the series editor, I was excited to be part of such an innovative endeavor. At that time there were few professional books available for teachers who wanted to bring young adult literature into their classrooms, and Heinemann was the first publisher making a concerted effort to fill this need. Seventeen years and many books later, under the direction of Heinemann Executive Editor Lisa Luedeke, the series continues to inform and assist teachers at the middle school, high school, and college levels as they read with and teach to their students the best works that the field of young adult literature has to offer.

The Heinemann YAL Series takes another step forward with the book you hold in your hands. This subseries on teaching the works of specific young adult authors is designed to help you incorporate young adult literature into your curriculum, providing ideas and lessons that you may use and offering examples of classroom-tested student work, lesson plans, and discussion as an impetus to designing your own lessons and developing your own ideas in accordance with your students' needs.

The first two books in this series are *Teaching the Selected Works of Robert Cormier* and *Teaching the Selected Works of Mildred D. Taylor.* Next, Heinemann will publish books in 2007 that focus on the works of Katherine Paterson and Walter Dean Myers; later, books on teaching selected works of Chris Crutcher and Gary Paulsen will follow.

Over the years, many teachers in my graduate young adult literature classes have asked me how to convince administrators and parents that young adult literature is worthy of a place in the curriculum alongside the classics and other commonly taught literary works. In response I have shown them how to write rationales for specific books, how to design lesson plans and units that satisfy state and national standards, how to deal with censorship, and how to become connoisseurs of young adult literature themselves. I hope that the books in this subseries, by focusing on specific authors of young adult literature and highlighting the successful work of teachers with this genre, will inspire confidence in you to bring these extraordinary works into your curriculum, not just as a bridge to the classics, but as literary works in their own right.

VIRGINIA R. MONSEAU

Teaching the Selected Works of Mildred D. Taylor

Chris Crowe

HEINEMANN
PORTSMOUTH, NH

Heinemann
A division of Reed Elsevier Inc.
361 Hanover Street
Portsmouth, NH 03801–3912
www.heinemann.com

Offices and agents throughout the world

CIP data is on file at the Library of Congress.
ISBN-13: 978-0-325-00789-2
ISBN-10: 0-325-00789-6

Editor: Virginia Monseau
Production: Vicki Kasabian
Cover design: Night & Day Design
Typesetter: Tom Allen/Pear Graphic Design
Manufacturing: Steve Bernier

Printed in the United States of America on acid-free paper
11 10 09 08 07 VP 1 2 3 4 5

For Ken Donelson

CONTENTS

Additional material can be found on the Heinemann website

ACKNOWLEDGMENTS

This project would not have been completed without generous support from the College of Humanities and the Department of English at Brigham Young University, which provided me with a wonderful graduate research assistant, Nathan Phillips. I'm grateful to Nate for his good work on this project. Once again, the Harold B. Lee Library and their Interlibrary Loan Office at BYU provided invaluable and prompt support, and I remain in their debt.

Of course, I am most grateful to Mildred D. Taylor for writing the kinds of books that educate and inspire and that richly reward those who reread them.

Mildred D. Taylor

ildred D. Taylor's birth, in Jackson, Mississippi, on September 13, 1943, was sandwiched between two significant periods in U.S. history, the Great Depression and World War II. When Taylor began her writing career thirty years later, both periods would provide essential background material for her books. Today, she is one of America's best-known authors of historical fiction for young readers, and although two of her stories are set in the late nineteenth and early twentieth centuries, she draws heavily from the history of 1930s and 1940s for most of her fiction.

As important as American history is to the work of Mildred D. Taylor, the soul of her stories springs from two more-personal sources: her family and racism. Much has been written about the influence of Taylor's father on her life and storytelling, but equally important are her mother, grandparents, aunts, uncles, and cousins. Her extended family has always provided support and encouragement for Taylor, but they also have contributed the basis for characters and plots in her novels. More important, though, the *idea* of family is a central thematic concern in all of Taylor's books. It's impossible to read any one of the Logan stories without understanding better the benefits of a close-knit, loving family.

In addition to the influence of family on Taylor's writing, her experience of being born in the racist South, being raised in a segregated country, and being among the first African American students to integrate American public schools impressed upon her the injustice of racism and segregation, and that injustice—in all its complexities—surfaces in every Taylor story. In her acceptance speech for the 1997 ALAN Award, Taylor revealed both her authorial intention as well as the impact of family and racism on her writing:

> From *Song of the Trees* to *The Well* I have attempted to present a true picture of life in America as older members of my family remember it, and as I remember it in the days before the civil rights movement. In all of the books I have recounted not only the joy of growing up in a large and supportive family, but my own feelings of being faced with segregation and bigotry. (1998, 3)

For Taylor, there is a strong connection between family and racism. Her stories make clear how a large and supportive family is essential if one is to survive and perhaps even overcome the obstacles of segregation and bigotry.

Mildred D. Taylor was the second child born to native Mississippians Wilbert Lee Taylor and Deletha Marie Davis Taylor. Her extended family had been in Mississippi for at least three generations, and on her father's side, the family traced its Mississippi heritage to Mildred's great-grandfather, the son of an African American slave woman and a white slave owner in Alabama. As a young man, Taylor's great-grandfather had a falling out with his white father and ran away from home, eventually settling in Mississippi in the 1880s. There, through hard work and his sharp wit, determination, and courage, he was able to purchase land, a remarkable achievement for a poor young African American man in the racist South at the end of the nineteenth century. Holding on to the land was not easy for the great-grandfather or his children and grandchildren, but despite a variety of economic and social hardships, her great-grandfather and his family were able to retain the land, even after a time add to it. Many of his descendants were raised on that property, and the land remains in Taylor's family to this day.

About a month after Taylor's birth in 1943, her father, who had been working for a trucking company in Jackson, quit his job because of a racist incident and left Mississippi in search of work in the more tolerant North. Leaving Mississippi, the home of his father, grandfather, and extended family, was difficult, but Wilbert Taylor was determined to raise his two daughters in a place where the color of their skin wouldn't limit their potential or threaten their lives. A week after arriving in

Toledo, Ohio, he found employment in a factory, and his wife and daughters joined him in Toledo shortly before the Christmas holidays. With both parents working, Taylor's family soon had enough money to purchase a home, and in the years following, that house became a way station and gathering place for cousins, uncles, and aunts who themselves were migrating from the racist South to the North.

Even though Wilbert Taylor hated the oppressive Jim Crow culture of the South, he loved his homeland and the family who had remained in Mississippi, so throughout his life, he regularly took his wife and daughters to visit family and friends in the state they had left. He even hoped that in time he would be able to move back to the home established by his grandfather. In her Newbery Award acceptance speech, Taylor explained her father's dream of returning home:

> He had never forgotten the feel of the soft red earth. He had never forgotten the goodness of walking on acres of his own land, of knowing that land had a history that stretched back over many generations. There, next to the house which my great-grandfather had built, he hoped to build his own house, surrounding it with flowers and fruit trees, with horses and cows, tending his own land with the love he had felt for it as a boy. (1977, 409)

Unfortunately, Wilbert Taylor died in 1976 before he was able to realize his dream of moving back to the land of his birth.

For young Mildred, the frequent family trips to Mississippi taught her to love the place as her father had, but they also acquainted her with family and Jim Crow culture. When her extended family came together during Taylor's visits to the South, her father and uncles would hold forth as storytellers, entertaining the children and other relatives with lively tales from their family history. At the feet of these men, Mildred learned about her rich heritage in Mississippi and how that heritage was affected by racism.

> There were stories of the great-grandfather, born the son of a white Alabama plantation owner and a black woman, then a slave. There were stories about how the great-grandfather had made his way into Mississippi and had accumulated land. There were stories about the Indian great-grandmother who died young. There were stories about the brash young men who were my great-uncles, stories about cousins and neighbors and chain gangs and clashes with the white law. But the stories that delighted me most were the stories told about my father and his brothers and sister growing up on the family land. (Taylor 1990, 741)

When she began writing about the fictional Logan family, the hours she had spent listening to the men in her family telling stories would provide her with both the narrative tradition and the material for writing stories of her own.

In addition to family gatherings and storytelling sessions during these visits, Taylor and her sister sometimes experienced the day-to-day existence of her Mississippi cousins. If school was in session, they would attend classes in the same small community school her father had attended. In summers, they would go into the fields and help pick cotton. Her father encouraged these activities because he wanted his daughters to experience, in a small way, what life had been like for him and his wife. He knew that such experiences would help his daughters appreciate the comfort and freedom they enjoyed in suburban Ohio. Taylor wrote that her father explained to them "that without understanding the loss of liberty in the South, we couldn't appreciate the liberty of the North" (1988, 272).

Taylor enjoyed a pleasant childhood in Toledo, growing up surrounded by various relatives who at one time or another shared her parents' home. She was an avid reader, an excellent student, and a young woman who was keenly aware of the world around her. When she was in fifth grade, her family moved to a larger house in Toledo, and she went from attending an elementary school where most of her classmates were African American to a fifth-grade class where she had few African American peers. In 1954, the year in which the U.S. Supreme Court would declare that racially segregated schools violated the Constitution, Taylor was the only African American student in her sixth-grade class. It was that year that she began to feel an intense pressure to succeed because she feared that if she didn't, her failure would reflect negatively on all African Americans. This fierce determination to succeed also led her to set goals that would direct the rest of her life. Phyllis Fogelman, Taylor's editor at Dial Books, wrote that Taylor made many important decisions about her future while she was still young:

> The first, of course, was about writing—made when she was nine or ten. She was also determined to see the world; at sixteen she decided she would join the Peace Corps upon graduation from college. She wanted very much to be sent to Ethiopia, and from then until she was graduated from the University of Toledo, she devoured everything she could get her hands on about the Peace Corps and Ethiopia. (1977, 412)

After four years as a successful student, including membership in the honor society and leadership in student government and the school newspaper, Taylor graduated from Scott High School in 1961. She enrolled at the University of

Toledo hoping to major in creative writing or journalism, but her father encouraged her to study something practical, so Taylor declared herself an English major
who would also certify to work as a high school teacher. She graduated in 1965
with a bachelor's degree in education.

Upon graduating from college, Taylor achieved one of her longtime goals: to
serve in the Peace Corps. Following several weeks of training at the University of
Utah and in Tuba City, Arizona, Taylor was sent to Yirga 'Alem, Ethiopia, where she
taught English and history for two years. After her release from the Peace Corps,
she spent another year working as a recruiter and instructor for that organization
before enrolling at the University of Colorado to earn a master's degree in journalism. She completed her degree in 1969 and stayed on at the university for two
additional years working as a study skills program coordinator.

Eager to begin her writing career, Taylor moved to Los Angeles in 1971. She
found undemanding work that provided enough money to live on and that
allowed her to conserve her creative energy for writing in the evenings and on
weekends. After almost two years of steady rejection, Taylor discovered that using
the storytelling tradition of her family and writing stories based on her family's
experiences in Mississippi released her own natural writing voice. In October
1973, she entered a book manuscript in a contest sponsored by the Council on
Interracial Books for Children. Her story won the contest and was purchased for
publication by Dial Books. That novella, *Song of the Trees*, was published in the
spring of 1975 and marked the beginning of Taylor's career as a writer of historical fiction for young readers. A year later, Dial published her second book, *Roll of
Thunder, Hear My Cry*, which won the 1977 Newbery Medal and immediately
established her as one of the most prominent contemporary authors in the United
States. That success also confirmed what Taylor had learned when writing *Song of
the Trees*: her best stories relied on a first-person narrator and on the true-life history of her family in Mississippi.

Taylor has published seven more award-winning books: *Let the Circle Be
Unbroken* (1981); *The Friendship* (1987); *The Gold Cadillac* (1987); *The Road to
Memphis* (1990); *Mississippi Bridge* (1990); *The Well* (1995); and *The Land* (2001).
She plans to write one more novel, tentatively titled *Logan*, in the saga of the
Logan family. *Logan* will take the family from post–World War II Mississippi to the
North and will complete the family history that begins in *The Land*, the story of
Paul Edward Logan's growing up, purchase of land in Mississippi in the 1880s, and
establishment of the homestead for the Logan family.

When she first made up her mind to become a writer, Mildred D. Taylor could not have imagined the success she would eventually achieve. In addition to the Newbery Medal, her books have won many prestigious prizes, including the Coretta Scott King Award, *Boston Globe–Horn Book* Award, Jane Addams Book Award, Scott O'Dell Award, and Christopher Award. In addition to the recognition for individual books, she has also been honored for the body of her work: in 1997, she received the ALAN Award for her contributions to young adult literature; in 2003, she was awarded the inaugural NSK Neustadt Prize for Children's Literature; and in 2004, the governor of Mississippi, Haley Barbour, declared April 2, Mildred D. Taylor Day.

Despite her many awards and widespread recognition, Taylor remains a humble and fiercely private person, rarely granting interviews or making public appearances. The honors have not puffed up her ego, but they do signify the importance of her work. Taylor is one of the few authors in American literature to have so successfully presented a personal glimpse into the lives of African Americans of the past. As she said in her ALAN Award acceptance speech, "I have tried to present not only a history of my family, but the effect of racism, not only on the victims of racism but to the racists themselves" (1998, 3). More than mere historical fiction, her books help young readers see—and feel—the evils associated with racism and have done much to teach modern Americans about the effects of segregation and prejudice. That is why the books of Mildred D. Taylor are worth reading and studying, today more than ever.

Works Cited

Fogelman, Phyllis J. 1977. "Mildred D. Taylor." *Horn Book Magazine* 53 (4): 410–14.

Taylor, Mildred D. 1977. "Newbery Medal Acceptance Speech." *Horn Book Magazine* 53 (4) (August): 401–9.

———. 1988. "Mildred D. Taylor." In *Something About the Author Autobiography Series*, vol. 5, edited by Adele Sarkissian, 267–86. Detroit: Gale Research Company.

———. 1990. "Growing Up with Stories." *Booklist*, December 1: 740–41.

———. 1998. "Acceptance Speech for the 1997 ALAN Award." *The ALAN Review* 25 (Spring): 2–3. [Also at http://scholar.lib.vt.edu/ejournals/ALAN/spring98/taylor.html.]

Let the Circle Be Unbroken
Using Literature Circles to Teach the Novels of Mildred D. Taylor

I firmly believe that there is something inherently good in literature, that there is some intangible essence that's transmitted to those who read and appreciate great books. Because of my unwavering faith in the basic good-for-you-ness of literature, during my first few years as a high school English teacher, I used the castor oil approach in my eleventh-grade American literature class, telling my students that although their encounter with American literature might be bitter and unpleasant, it would, in the long run, be good for them. Every year, we dutifully plowed through our anthology: William Bradford, Jonathan Edwards, William Byrd, Thomas Paine, Washington, Jefferson, Franklin, Washington Irving, James Fenimore Cooper, Edgar Allan Poe, and on and on. The students resisted at first, but numbed by the combined effects of my lectures and their reading, they eventually gave in to the inexorable lull of literature class. In my heart of hearts, I believed the numbing was good for them; it was a benign paralysis that one day they would thank me for.

Fortunately, after years of being beaten with the obvious and undeniable facts that my students despised most of our reading assignments and that an ever-dwindling number even bothered to read them, my head overruled my heart of hearts. Something was not right about my students' abhorrence of reading in general and American literature in particular. Students should like to read. I like to read. So why, I asked myself, did my students hate reading? And what could I do, should I do, to change their attitudes toward reading and literature (because, after all, kids inevitably connect and condemn the two—guilt by association)?

That's when the epiphany struck. While honestly reflecting on my own initial encounters with the American Literary Canon, I recalled, dimly and reluctantly, that I had not enjoyed much of what I read. In college, the four-year force feeding of Great Literature killed my appetite for reading, and by the end of my undergraduate literature studies, I pretty much hated to read anything. It wasn't until the second semester of my first year of teaching that I began to read for pleasure again (and, no, it wasn't *Wieland* or *Paradise Lost*).

When I considered what I read for pleasure, the books that fed my reading desire, I realized that even I, an English teacher, did not read "Sinners in the Hands of an Angry God" for fun. No, I read Tom Clancy's *Red Storm Rising* and Robert Cormier's *The Chocolate War*, Chris Crutcher's *Running Loose* and contemporary short stories by Raymond Chandler, T. Coraghessan Boyle, Eudora Welty, Flannery O'Connor, and others; not exactly the literary pantheon presented in my American lit book. So I asked myself (at this point, my classes were going so badly that I was regularly talking to myself; it was the only dialogue I could count on in my deader-than-a-doornail classroom): what was it that made my personal reading pleasurable?

The answer was obvious: I enjoyed my reading because I chose it myself, because I didn't need a teacher or professor to translate it for me, and because I didn't have to answer to anyone about what I read—no papers, no tests, no classroom "discussions." I read for me, first and foremost.

The light began to dawn. Why (yes, I asked myself once again) should I expect things of my students that I didn't expect of myself? And did it do any good to expose my students to the Great American Literary Canon if they learned nothing more than to hate it—or even worse, to hate all reading?

Convinced that there still was something inherently good in reading great American literature, I realized my approach had been wrong, wrong, wrong, and I decided then and there to change my teaching ways, to transform myself from a literary pre-Christmas Scrooge to a post-Christmas Scrooge. I exchanged my castor oil approach for a milk-before-meat approach, an approach that took one curricular step backward in return for, I hoped, two steps forward.

It was a dramatic change, one that surely would have drawn the censure of my colleagues, my department chair, and my principal if they had found me out. Casting caution to the wind, I broke the unwritten rules of American Literature. I circumvented the district curriculum. I chucked the trusty American literature anthology out the window.

Literally. (Or literarily, as the case may be.)

And that got my students' attention.

"Don't try this at home," I warned. "And don't tell anyone, but we're about to embark on a Grand Experiment."

A few eyebrows perked up.

"We're not going to be using that old book for a while. We might come back to it—might—but first we're going to try something different, something better" (I hoped).

I then unveiled the details of the Grand Experiment, the bold rule-breaking change of course. I talked to my students about educational theory, about learners being responsible for their own learning. I explained the importance of relevance, independent study, collaborative learning. And finally, I read to them the American Literature Objectives from our school district's curriculum guide.

Then I shut up and invited them to suggest their own objectives for our American literature class.

The room fell silent while my students struggled to determine whether I was serious or just crazy. After some moments, a few spoke up tentatively. Soon the entire class joined in. They wanted to read and understand the classics. They also said, to my barely contained delight, that they wanted to write better, to read more effectively, to understand grammar, to understand the workings of literature, and—ta-da!—*to enjoy reading*.

"Enjoy reading. That's exactly what I want you to do too," I said (no longer to myself). "And that's exactly what we're going to do."

Phase 1 of the Grand Experiment was dedicated to helping them enjoy reading. They had to choose an American novel, any novel—sci-fi, romance, horror, western, classic—and read it. I didn't care how long, how serious, how classic it was. But for one week, all we did was read.

The next week, I gave them a list of tasks to complete within the following two weeks: a brief written reaction to their book; two informal book talks to the class about their novel, one at midpoint and one after the book was finished; a personal vocabulary list from their reading; and finally, a brief quiz covering literary terms as they applied to their novel.

The students dug into their books and assignments. Their oral reports revealed their pleasure at being free to read what they wanted. Several students read two books, and a girl who had never before read a book actually finished one. (Soon after that, she read three more, including *The Grapes of Wrath*.)

Phase 2 of the Grand Experiment had more structure. I book-talked five American novels (*The Great Gatsby, To Kill a Mockingbird, The Adventures of Tom Sawyer, The Scarlet Letter,* and *The Grapes of Wrath*) that covered a fairly broad range of reading interests and abilities. After the book talks, I asked my students to select one of the five that seemed most interesting to them, and divided the class into five groups. Each group would read and study the novel they had selected.

They had three weeks to read their novel and complete the various tasks associated with it. Each group met once or twice a week to discuss a series of general plot/analysis questions about their book. They also had to view available AV material about the book and its author and prepare an oral presentation explaining their novel to their classmates who hadn't read it. My classes had never gone so well. Many times during the Grand Experiment, the discussions and study groups went so well that I felt—and probably was—obsolete. My formerly dull and dead classroom came alive with talk and debate about literature.

At the end of our rule-breaking Grand Experiment, the great majority of my students admitted that they enjoyed reading, even reading some of the American classics. We then reapproached our anthology, and this time the students read more willingly, more perceptively, and with more pleasure. They didn't like everything, of course, but they felt free and able to explain why they didn't. Class discussions weren't always strikingly stimulating, but they were better, much better, than my lonely monologues.

Breaking the rules of the traditional approach to American literature reminded me of another, more basic and more important rule, a rule that is one of the best things we English teachers have going for us: *given the right circumstances, most people like to read.* Once we remind our students of that principle and allow them the freedom and opportunity to rediscover it for themselves, we're much more able—and they're better prepared—to take on the classics.

So what does my struggle to learn to teach American literature—or any literature—have to do with the books of Mildred D. Taylor? Yes, her novels fall comfortably into the realm of American literature, and her Newbery Medal book, *Roll of Thunder,*

Hear My Cry, has reached a sort of classic status in secondary schools. But how can these books be used productively in a secondary English or reading course?

I'm suggesting that Taylor's books offer a wonderful opportunity for focused literature circles. Literature circles are classroom or after-school activities involving clusters of readers who meet together regularly to discuss a common text. Harvey Daniels, one of the leading advocates of literature circles, defines the approach by listing its twelve essential ingredients:

1. Students select their own books to read.

2. Students are placed in small groups based on their reading selections.

3. Different groups read different books.

4. Groups meet on a regular schedule to discuss their reading.

5. Students use their own notes to guide group reading and discussion.

6. Students generate their own discussion topics.

7. Group discussions are natural conversations about the reading.

8. Sometimes, groups may operate using specific, rotating roles.[1]

9. The teacher is a facilitator, not an instructor or group member.

10. Student self-evaluation and teacher observation determine a group's success.

11. The groups operate with a spirit of playfulness and fun.

12. When the books are finished, students share their reading experience with their classmates. (2002, 18–26)

Literature circles, by design, exist to stimulate natural, student-initiated discussion about a text. By participating in literature circles, students learn, through practice and models, how real readers operate before, during, and after reading a book. Circles are best used when reading is organized around a common theme or historical period. They also work well when instruction is focused on a particular author, especially if that author has a number of books to choose from. For more detailed information, see *Literature Circles: Voice and Choice in Book Clubs and Reading Groups* (Daniels 2002) and other print and Internet sources listed in Appendix A.

Dena G. Beeghly (2005) offers suggestions on how to set up and conduct electronic literature circles. Though her focus is on adult students, her method can easily be adapted for use with secondary students. E-literature circles might also be an excellent way to extend the classroom literature discussion. With a little coaching, students could be encouraged to use the Internet to continue their reading conversations with classmates after school.

For teachers interested in differentiated instruction, Taylor's body of work offers an excellent opportunity for classes of students with widely varying reading interests and abilities to have a common, unifying reading experience without reading the same book. The literature circles unit might be called The Logan Family Saga or Reading Mildred D. Taylor or Family and Overcoming Jim Crow or any other thematic title, but regardless of the label, every student in class would read one of Taylor's books. The class can have up to nine different reading circles, each group using a Taylor book that is appropriate for their reading and interest level. Taylor's publications offer something for almost every reader, ranging from easy-to-read, illustrated stories (*The Friendship*, *The Gold Cadillac*, and *Mississippi Bridge*) to novellas (*Song of the Trees* and *The Well*) to fully developed novels (*Roll of Thunder, Hear My Cry*, *Let the Circle Be Unbroken*, *The Road to Memphis*, and *The Land*). Even within these three groups of books, the reading levels—especially if determined by content—provide a range of material to accommodate most any readers. For example, among the illustrated stories, *The Gold Cadillac* is the least disturbing. It still presents unvarnished racism, but no one dies, and no one is physically injured.

To begin the Mildred D. Taylor literature circles, you, the teacher, would book-talk each of Taylor's nine books and then allow the students to sort themselves into the literature circle they prefer. Of course, you might have to set some limits regarding the number of students in a group, and a few students may need to be directed to the circle that will be best for them. It's likely that *Roll of Thunder* may have been taught in prior grades, and if so, you might elect to eliminate that novel from the list of choices. Other of her books might also be eliminated based on the demographics and needs of a particular class. The circles can still be effective even if you use fewer than all nine of Taylor's books.

The day-to-day class work is up to you. Some class periods may be devoted solely to reading, while others may be completely filled with activities and discussion. You can determine what each group will do as it reads its book, but Appendix D offers some generic questions that all students can apply to their reading. Of course, creative teachers—and their students—will be able to come up with many productive and interesting learning activities to complement and extend the reading experience.

Perhaps the most exciting aspects of a Mildred D. Taylor literature circle are the opportunities it provides for intergroup and whole-class discussion. Because all of Taylor's books are about one generation or another of the Logan family and all the stories are set within an eighty-year span, the various reading groups will have many opportunities for intergroup discussions. Students reading *The Friendship*, for example, can talk with students who are reading *The Land* to get some background information on the relationship between Tom Bee and John Wallace. Students reading *Roll of Thunder, Hear My Cry* might talk with classmates reading *Song of the Trees* to learn more about the tree-cutting incident referred to in *Roll of Thunder* or ask students reading *The Well* to give some insight into the childhood of David Logan or the evil Simms family.

In addition to character connections, the various groups can also find parallel thematic and historical elements in their respective Taylor books. Every one of Taylor's stories in some way shows the importance of family, the consequences of racism, and the value of land ownership. Individual reading groups can share with the class how their particular story presents one of those themes, or two groups can meet together to discuss the parallel themes in the novels they're reading. Besides connecting themes, students might also find common historical elements. For example, *The Land* and *The Well* take place on either side of the turn of the twentieth century when the South was still trying to come out from under the failed Reconstruction of segregated society. *Mississippi Bridge, Song of the Trees, The Friendship, Let the Circle Be Unbroken*, and *Roll of Thunder, Hear My Cry* are set during the Great Depression. The common settings among these stories will provide students opportunities to discuss American history and to review how the historical setting influences the plot of their stories. (See the list of suggested activities in Appendix E for other assignments that could be used for intergroup or whole-class discussion and study.)

The focused literature circles I'm suggesting will yield many benefits. By the end of a literature circle unit on the books of Mildred D. Taylor, students will come away with a better understanding of many of Taylor's books, of course, but they'll also have a keener insight into the effects of racism on its victims and its perpetrators. They'll know American history, particularly the 1930s, like they never have before. They'll appreciate the struggles African Americans and other marginalized groups have faced while trying to earn their rightful places in American society.

They'll understand how vital it is, how vital it has always been, for American citizens to own property. They'll see the importance of resisting oppression in acceptable ways and appreciate how important a strong family can be in helping people stand up to difficulties. And perhaps most important, if the unit is set up and managed well, by the end of the reading, students will have greater confidence in their own reading abilities and a realization that sometimes reading can be a pleasure.

Experiences like this will give students the confidence and skills necessary to tackle the other literary works they encounter in secondary school; these experiences will be instrumental in turning young people into lifelong readers.

The chapters that follow treat each of Taylor's major books individually and provide basic background material for each book that teachers can adapt for single-book study or for use in literature circles. The discussion of each book is followed by lists of questions (Prereading Questions and Writing Topics, Questions for Writing and Discussion, and Making Text-to-Text Connections to Other Stories) and by a list of print and Internet resources to support or extend instruction and literature circle activities. The appendices at the end of the book contain a wide variety of additional information and material that will be helpful in teaching Mildred D. Taylor's books.

Note

1. The roles may vary depending on course objectives, student abilities, and teacher direction. Here are some examples of task/roles that may be assigned: plot mapper, discussion leader, vocabulary guru, theme detective, illustrator, Dr. Who, note taker. Teachers and/or students can come up with roles that are appropriate to the group's needs or goals.

Works Cited

Beeghly, Dena G. 2005. "It's About Time: Using Electronic Literature Discussion Groups with Adult Learners." *Journal of Adolescent and Adult Literacy* 49 (1) (September): 12–21.

Daniels, Harvey. 2002. *Literature Circles: Voice and Choice in Book Clubs and Reading Groups.* Portland, ME: Stenhouse.

The Land
Family History and Reconstruction

Synopsis

Taylor's most recent novel, *The Land* (2001), is the prequel to her Logan family saga, thus making this a logical starting point for the reading and discussion of her novels. *The Land* is the story of Paul-Edward Logan, a character based on Taylor's own great-grandfather. The novel is divided into two sections, "Childhood" and "Manhood." A brief epilogue titled "Legacy" concludes the story. The novel, Taylor's first in six years, won many awards, including the 2002 Coretta Scott King Award and the 2002 Scott O'Dell Award.

Setting
Part I: Georgia, 1870s
Part II: Mississippi, 1880s

Characters
Paul-Edward Logan, narrator
Mitchell Thomas, son of the plantation horse trainer; Paul's best friend
Edward Logan, Paul's father

Hammond Logan, Paul's half brother
George Logan, Paul's half brother
Robert Logan, Paul's half brother, the same age as Paul
Deborah, a former slave, Paul's mother
Cassie Logan, Paul's sister
Christian Waverly, local white boy, classmate of Robert's
Percy Waverly, local white boy, classmate of Robert's
Ray Sutcliffe, racist horse owner
Miz Hattie Crenshaw, white woman who befriends Paul and Mitchell
Jessup, white boss at the lumber camp
Luke Sawyer, mercantile owner in Vicksburg
J. T. Hollenback, northern owner of the land Paul covets
Caroline Perry, a local girl who becomes Mitchell's wife, then Paul's
Sam Perry, her father, a healer
Rachel Perry, her mother
Nathan Perry, her younger brother
Charles Jamison, a lawyer and local landowner
Wade Jamison, his son
Fillmore Granger, a local landowner
Harlan Granger, his son
Tom Bee, a lumber camp worker, friend of Mitchell's
John Wallace, his white protégé
Digger Wallace, John's drunken older brother
Horace Avery, friend of Tom Bee's hired to help clear the Logan land

Plot Summary

The story begins with Paul-Edward Logan, age nine, living on his father's plantation in Georgia. Even though Paul is the son of a slave woman, when he is young he is in most ways the equal of his white half brothers: he's educated, he eats in the kitchen of the big house, he is recognized by all as one of the son's of the master. An early antagonist is Mitchell Thomas, the son of the plantation's black horse trainer. Mitchell is jealous of the privileged life led by Paul and he takes every available opportunity to torment Paul, usually by beating him. Knowing that his father won't defend him and that he can't outfight Mitchell, Paul lands on a scheme that will end the beatings and at the same time help him learn to defend himself. He offers to teach Mitchell to read and write if Mitchell will teach him how to fight. Mitchell accepts the bargain, and in time one boy learns to read and write, the other to fight, and the two boys become close friends.

A key turning point in Paul's relationship with his father comes when his father tries to prepare him for life as a person of color in the racist culture of Georgia of the 1870s. On Christmas Eve, Paul-Edward is provoked into a fight with his half brother Robert and the two Waverly boys, and instead of supporting Paul, who was clearly in the right, his father whips him. He explains to his furious son that even though he is the son of a prominent plantation owner and even though he looks white, he is still subject to the Jim Crow laws of the South. When he's older, fighting with a white person would likely get him lynched, his father explains, so it's essential that Paul never forget this lesson. "You've got to learn, Paul, and you've got to learn now, you don't ever hit a white man. Ever. . . . You keep that smart mouth and you're going to end up getting yourself killed. You don't hit a white man and you don't sass a white man" (82–83). Better a whipping from his own father than death from a lynch mob. Unfortunately for father and son, Paul is too hardheaded and perhaps too naive to accept this lesson, and rather than learn from the experience, he begins to resent his father and the white boys who started the trouble.

The next important event in Paul's life comes when he is fourteen. He and Mitchell accompany Paul's father to a horse show in Texas, and while there, Paul disobeys his father by riding a horse in a local horse race. Paul wins the race but is denied his wages by the horse's white owner, Ray Sutcliffe. Paul had planned to use the money to strike out on his own because he knows that having disobeyed his father he will be severely beaten; rather than take another beating at the hands of his own father, he decides to run away. Paul convinces Mitchell, who's been having troubles with his own father, to go with him, but before they leave, Mitchell jumps Sutcliffe, hits him, and takes Paul's rightful wages from him. Now the boys have no choice but to run away.

Part II of the novel, "Manhood," begins with Paul and Mitchell, now young men, working in a lumber camp in Mississippi. Since running away from Texas, Paul and Mitchell have worked for almost two years for Miz Hattie Crenshaw on her land near Laurel, Mississippi. When circumstances on the Crenshaw land change because of Miz Crenshaw's daughters' marriages, Paul and Mitchell strike out on their own, Mitchell looking to enjoy his freedom, Paul hoping to find a way to achieve his dream of owning land. First they work in a turpentine camp, but the work and the people are too unpleasant. Paul teaches, does carpentry, and trains horses from time to time, but more of the work Paul and Mitchell find is in lumber camps. Paul tires of the lumber camps, and the two leave the camp and for the first time in their lives, split up. Paul goes to Vicksburg to work as a furniture maker for Luke Sawyer; Mitchell works at a lumber camp not far away.

On his way to Vicksburg, Paul comes across a piece of land owned by northerner J. T. Hollenback and determines that somehow, someday, he will own it. After more than a year of making furniture, Paul strikes a deal with Fillmore Granger to clear forty acres of Granger's land and give the lumber to Granger. In return, when the land is cleared, Granger will transfer the ownership of the forty acres to Paul. Mitchell returns to help Paul in the work; Mitchell also marries Caroline Perry. Others come to help: Tom Bee, Nathan Perry, and two white boys, John Wallace and Wade Jamison. Paul's plan is to sell the cleared land and use the money and his savings to purchase the Hollenback land he covets. When the land is nearly cleared, Digger Wallace murders Mitchell; before he dies, Mitchell makes Paul promise to marry Caroline and raise their baby as his own son. Soon after Mitchell's death, when the land is finally cleared, Granger reneges on the deal, leaving Paul and Caroline with no land. When Paul is most desperate, he writes to his sister, Cassie, hoping that she'll be able to help. Days later, just before the opportunity for the Hollenback land will pass, Paul's half-brother Robert appears on the scene with money Cassie received from selling their mother's land. Paul is able to purchase his dream land and then marries Caroline.

"Legacy," the epilogue, brings the story full circle. Paul and Caroline have four sons, and by using borrowed money, the couple is able to purchase an additional two hundred acres of land from the Jamisons. When his oldest boys are teenagers, Paul takes his children back to Georgia to meet their white uncles and white grandfather. They arrive at the old plantation not long after Edward Logan has slipped into a coma. He revives long enough to see Paul and to listen to what Paul's done with his life.

The book concludes with a note from Mildred D. Taylor that briefly explains how *The Land* parallels the true story of her own great-grandfather and their extended family.

Discussion

The Land introduces the themes, issues, and some characters that continue throughout the rest of the Logan saga. For example, in *The Friendship* (1987) we see the end of the relationship between old Tom Bee and the adult John Wallace. John Wallace and Harlan Granger appear as boys in *The Land*; as adults in other Logan stories, they function as central antagonists. Future allies of the Logan family, Wade Jamison and Horace Avery, also make appearances in *The Land*. Paul and Mitchell work as character foils in *The Land* in a manner similar to the foil pairs of David Logan and Hammer Logan and Stacy Logan and T. J. Avery in other Logan stories; and the friendly white boy, Wade Jamison, foreshadows the character of Jeremy Simms, a white boy who befriends Cassie and her brothers in many of the Logan tales. Taylor also establishes the roots of other elements of the Logan saga in this prequel: the family history of slavery, the determination to keep the land, the constant threats from racists, and the economic challenges facing poor black families in the South. This most recent novel also echoes the two themes central to all of Taylor's stories. Paul-Edward Logan's determination to own land and his love of family are key traits passed on to his Logan heirs. The core values of *The Land*—how independence and survival depend on land ownership and how survival depends on a unified, loving family—are prominent in every one of Taylor's books.

Taylor adds two features to *The Land* that contain significantly more material than similar features in the other Logan books. Many of her books have brief acknowledgments, but the acknowledgments in this novel are the longest of any, and in addition to recognizing the importance of the stories from her extended family, emphasize the roles of her two uncles, James E. Taylor and Eugene Taylor, in the creation of many of her books. She also acknowledges the support of her longtime friend and editor, Phyllis J. Fogelman, who has worked with and encouraged Taylor from *The Song of the Trees* through *The Land*. Taylor's heartfelt and thoughtful gratitude suggest how much she values family and personal relationships, relationships that play key roles in her life and in her fiction. Taylor has often added author's notes to her books, usually in the front matter, but her note at the end of this novel contains the most personal and detailed material of anything she has published till now. The note makes clear connections between characters and story elements in the novel and real people and events in Taylor's family history; and for the first time, Taylor writes of a personal struggle to acquire and then hold on to precious land in the Rockies, a struggle she sees as similar in many ways to the efforts of her great-grandfather and his descendants to purchase and retain land in Mississippi. The acknowledgments and author's note frame the novel in Taylor's family history, and it is that personal sense of history that charges this story with such powerful emotion.

The novel is also imbued with the history of Reconstruction, the post–Civil War period from 1865 to 1877. Lincoln's Emancipation Proclamation and the North's eventual victory freed the slaves and suggested that they too would finally benefit from the freedoms and opportunities promised in the U. S. Constitution. The events in *The Land* show how racists found ways to circumvent the Emancipation Proclamation and the Fourteenth and the Fifteenth Amendments, denying African Americans the basic privileges of democracy and keeping them in political and economic bondage. Even though Paul-Edward is the son of a white landowner in Georgia, he is not allowed to eat at his father's table when white visitors are present; he is not allowed to attend school with his white half brothers; and he is not a legitimate heir to his father's land. Perhaps the most painful event of all is the brutal lesson Paul-Edward learns at the hand of his own father. When Paul-Edward fights with his white half-brother Robert and the two Waverly boys, his father gives him a vicious whipping, one designed to teach young Paul-Edward that he must never violate the basic codes of the segregationist South, because any violation might easily result in his death. These Jim Crow restrictions are historically accurate and were even harsher for southern African American men and women who lived in circumstances that were less fortunate than Paul-Edward's during the Reconstruction period.

Prereading Questions and Writing Topics

(Also see the prereading activities in Appendix C.)

1. What are some of the earliest family stories you know? Find a story from your earliest ancestor and share it.

2. Imagine life in the racist South immediately after the Civil War. What kinds of problems might confront a boy whose mother is a former slave and whose father is a white plantation owner?

3. Immediately after the Civil War, did life for newly freed slaves in the South get better or worse? Find some examples to support your answer.

4. When disciplining their children, parents often use the expression, "This hurts me more than it hurts you." Put yourself in a parent's place and imag-

ine a circumstance in which you would have to do something very difficult, maybe even painful, in order to teach your child an essential lesson.

5. Imagine that you are a fourteen-year-old African American boy or girl in the South in the 1870s. You've lost your family and are now completely on your own. How would you survive? What could you do to provide food, clothing, and shelter for yourself?

6. What would you do if your father refused to allow you any of the privileges and opportunities your brothers and sisters enjoy?

Questions for Writing and Discussion

1. After reading the first two chapters, predict what will happen to Paul-Edward and to Mitchell.

2. In what ways is Paul-Edward naive? How might that character flaw complicate his life?

3. Explain the family dynamics that exist on the plantation where Paul-Edward lives.

4. How do the social codes (the Jim Crow segregationist policies) of this period affect Paul-Edward? His father? His white brothers?

5. Why does the white woman Miz Hattie Crenshaw agree to hide Paul-Edward and Mitchell? What kind of people would praise her for hiding the boys? What kind of people would condemn her for hiding the boys?

6. Look up the Reconstruction terms *scalawag* and *carpetbagger.* Which of these terms might best apply to J. T. Hollenback? Why?

7. Why is Fillmore Granger able to violate the agreement he had with Paul-Edward for the forty acres of land that Paul-Edward and his friends cleared?

8. Why is land ownership so important to Paul-Edward?

9. How do the various setbacks and tragedies he endures in the novel affect Paul-Edward?

10. Find at least three examples of deus ex machina (or "coincidences") that solve a problem for Paul-Edward. Are the events believable or do them seem too convenient? Explain your answers.

Making Text-to-Text Connections to Other Stories

1. Find another novel or story that is set in the Reconstruction period. How is that different from or similar to *The Land*?

2. Paul-Edward Logan is fair-skinned enough to pass for white. Why doesn't he take advantage of his mixed-race status? How is Paul-Edward similar to and different from Suzella Rankin, a mixed-race character in *Let the Circle Be Unbroken*?

3. At least twice in the novel, Edward Logan tells Paul-Edward to "use your head" (5, 87). In what circumstances does that same advice appear in *The Well* and *Roll of Thunder, Hear My Cry*? Why does Taylor use this advice so often?

4. Tom Bee is a central character in *The Friendship*. How has his relationship with John Wallace changed from their relationship in *The Land*? What might have caused the change?

5. Caroline tells the story of how her mother had her name stolen during slavery times. How is that story repeated in *The Well* and in *Roll of Thunder, Hear My Cry*? Which version seems most poignant or powerful? Why?

Additional Resources

Print Sources

Barney, William L. 2002. *The Civil War and Reconstruction*. New York: Oxford.

Berlin, Ira, Marc Favreau, and Steven F. Miller. 2000. *Remembering Slavery: African Americans Talk About Their Personal Experiences of Slavery and Emancipation*. New York: New Press and Library of Congress.

Bolden, Tonya. 2005. *Cause: Reconstruction America, 1863–1877.* New York: Knopf.

Chesnutt, Charles W. 1993. *The House Behind the Cedars.* New York: Penguin Classics.

Collier, Christopher, and James Lincoln Collier. 2000. *Reconstruction and the Rise of Jim Crow.* New York: Benchmark.

Greene, Meg. 2004. *Into the Land of Freedom: African Americans in Reconstruction.* New York: Lerner.

Hakim, Joy. 1994. *Reconstruction and Reform.* New York: Oxford.

Ham, Debra Newman. 1994. *The African American Mosaic: A Library of Congress Resource Guide for the Study of Black History and Culture.* Washington DC: Library of Congress.

———. 2000. *The African American Odyssey.* Washington DC: Library of Congress.

King, David C. 2003. *Civil War and Reconstruction.* New York: Wiley.

Lewis, David Levering, and Deborah Willis. 2005. *A Small Nation of People: W. E. B. DuBois and African American Portraits of Progress.* New York: Amistad/HarperCollins.

Peck, Richard. 2003. *The River Between Us.* New York: Dial.

Piper, Adrian. 1992. "Passing for White, Passing for Black." *Transition* 58: 4–32.

Schneider, Dean. 2006. "A Quest for Land During Reconstruction." *Book Links* 15 (3) (January): 40–43.

Twain, Mark. 2002. *Pudd'nhead Wilson and Those Extraordinary Twins.* New York: Modern Library.

Wilson, Diane Lee. 2005. *Black Storm Comin'.* New York: Margaret K. McElderry.

Wormser, Richard. 2003. *The Rise and Fall of Jim Crow.* New York: St. Martin's.

Internet Sites

"Born in Slavery: Slave Narratives from the Federal Writers' Project, 1936–1938." http://memory.loc.gov/ammem/snhtml/snhome.html.

Davis School District Language Arts, *The Land.* www.davis.k12.ut.us/curric /languagearts/grade8.html.

"From Slavery to Freedom: African American Pamphlet Collection." http://memory.loc.gov/ammem/aapchtml/aapchome.html.

"Homecoming: Sometimes I am Haunted by Memories of Red Dirt and Clay." www.pbs.org/itvs/homecoming/.

The Learning Page/Lesson Plans. http://memory.loc.gov/learn/lessons/theme .html.

"Reconstruction: Roads to Reunion." www.archives.gov/exhibits/treasures_of
_congress/page_13.html.

The Rise and Fall of Jim Crow. PBS. www.pbs.org/wnet/jimcrow/.

Web English Teacher: *The Land.* www.webenglishteacher.com/mtaylor.html.

Roll of Thunder, Hear My Cry
The Politics of Jim Crow

Synopsis

Roll of Thunder, Hear My Cry (1976) is Mildred D. Taylor's best-known and most widely read book. (According to a 2000 survey by *Publisher's Weekly*, it is one of the top one hundred best-selling children's books of all time.) The success of this second book and first full-length novel confirmed Taylor's decision to retell family stories with Cassie Logan as the narrator. Among its many awards is the 1977 Newbery Medal. Taylor dedicated the novel to her father, who died four months before the book was published.

Setting
Rural Mississippi, 1933

Characters
Cassie Logan, narrator, nine
Little Man (Clayton Chester) Logan, six
Stacey Logan, twelve
Christopher-John Logan, seven
Harlan Filmore Granger

Papa, David Logan, Cassie's father
Big Ma/Caroline, Papa's mother
Mama, Mary Logan, Cassie's mother
Hammer Logan, Cassie's uncle
T. J. Avery

Claude Avery
Mr. Samuel Berry
John Henry Berry
Deacon Berry
Mrs. Berry
Mr. Silas Lanier
Mr. Kaleb Wallace
Jeremy Simms
Lillian Jean Simms
Mary Lou Wellever
Moe Turner
Miss Daisy Crocker
Miss Davis
Mr. Wellever
Mr. L. T. Morrison
Mrs. Lanier

Joe Avery
Fannie Avery
Mr. Ted Grimes
Sam Tatum
Miz Claire Thompson
Mr. Jim Lee Barnett
Mrs. Barnett
Little Willie Wiggins
Mr. Wiggins
Clarence
Kaleb Wallace
R. W. Simms
Melvin Simms
Mr. Dewberry Wallace
Mr. Simms

Plot Summary

A sequel to *Song of the Trees*, *Roll of Thunder, Hear My Cry* is set one year later, 1933, and extends and enriches the Logan family story established in Taylor's first book. Cassie narrates this coming-of-age story, which covers a year's worth of trouble in her tiny Mississippi community.

To get to school every day, Cassie and her brothers face a one-hour walk on dusty farm roads. Their daily trek to and from school is complicated by a school bus for white children that careens past them at dangerous speeds, coating them with (depending on the season) dust or mud. Unlike the well-provisioned white school that the Logan children pass by every day, their school, Great Faith Elementary and Secondary School, suffers from decades of Jim Crow neglect.

The novel opens on the first day of school, and readers are introduced to Cassie and her brothers; Stacey's friend, T. J. Avery; and the enigmatic white boy who is attracted to the Logans, Jeremy Simms. As the children trudge to school, the white children's bus whizzes by, coating them with dust, but that is only the first indignity they'll face that day. At school, Miz Daisy Crocker announces with delight (which proves unwarranted) that this year the students will have textbooks. Little Man, a lover of books, is excited by the prospect of real school books, but his hopes are dashed when he receives his book, a beat up copy that, after being worn out in the white schools for twelve years, has been handed down to the "nigra" students. This insults the proper and studious Little Man, and he throws his book to the floor, refusing to use it. Cassie soon joins the boycott, and both children are whipped by Miz Crocker for their insubordination and ingratitude.

This educational inequity overlays an existing racial tension in the local community. That day, Cassie and her brothers learn something that T. J. and most of the adults in the area already know: a group of racist white vigilantes had recently burned three men from the Berry family because a white woman accused one of the Berrys of leering at her. The attack on the Berrys is the first violent racist act in the novel, and it marks the beginning of Cassie's awakening to the painful realities of the Jim Crow South.

Papa Logan, who had been away working for the railroad in Louisiana, soon appears on the scene accompanied by a huge black man, Mr. L. T. Morrison. Mr. Morrison, one of Papa's coworkers, injured a white man in a fight and Papa has brought him to Mississippi to save him from being killed by angry white men. The children eventually learn that Mr. Morrison is there for another reason: to protect the family from the marauding night men in Papa's absence.

At this point, the plot ramps up as conflicts begin to compound. The community-spirited Logans decide that the attack on the Berrys cannot go unchallenged, so they organize and spearhead a boycott of the Wallace store. Their blatant, though mild, "attack" on Jim Crow infuriates all the local racists, including the Wallaces and the area's richest and most influential citizen, Harlan Granger. Now, in addition to fearing attacks from night men, the Logans also must worry about losing their land. Uncle Hammer soon joins the family, and his brassy, confident manner only angers local racists even more. T. J. Avery adds yet another thread of conflict to the story as his underhanded ways cause problems for Stacey and eventually the entire Logan family.

Problems begin to surface in nearly every aspect of Logan life. T. J.'s cheating earns Stacey a whipping at school. Cassie has a humiliating run-in with a white girl, Lillian Simms, and Cassie's plan for revenge, while cunning and creative, adds tension to the story because of the possible repercussions. T. J.'s stories at the Wallace store get Mary Logan fired from her job at Great Faith Elementary and Secondary School, and the loss of her income puts the Logan land at risk. The family's situation grows even worse when late one night white men attack Papa, Mr. Morrison, and Stacey on their return from their shopping trip to Vicksburg. Papa is shot and has his leg broken, and his injuries prevent him from returning to work on the railroads. Thanks to the behind-the-scene machinations of Harlan Granger, the mortgage on the Logan land comes due when the family has no cash to pay for it.

Amid this turmoil, the novel's central catalytic conflict emerges. T. J.'s conniving has finally alienated him from the Logans and his other black friends, and desperate for attention, he turns to the most unlikely of "friends": Melvin and R. W. Simms, two of the meanest, most racist young men in the community. As the Logans battle to save their land, T. J. lands himself in a tragic mess. Melvin and R. W. convince him to come with them to rob the Barnett store, a robbery that ultimately results in the death of the store owner. Melvin and R. W. pin the crime on T. J. who, because he's black, has neither defense nor ally.

The recent "uppiteness" of the Logans and other blacks has inflamed many of the local whites, and T. J.'s "crime" ignites the powder keg of anger and retribution. Under cover of night, a lynch mob kidnaps T. J., takes him to Harlan Granger's place, beats him, and prepares to hang him. A thunderstorm adds to the ominous scene and it appears that T. J.'s doom is sealed until Papa and Mr. Morrison, informed by Cassie of the goings-on at the Granger place, come to the rescue. They manage to distract the mob from their murderous intentions by setting fire to the Logan cotton field, a fire that quickly spreads to Granger land. When he sees that his land is threatened, Mr. Granger orders the mob to leave T. J. with the sheriff and get into the fields and fight the fire. The Logans' actions spare T. J. at a great personal cost.

At the novel's end, Cassie surveys the burned fields, considers what poor T. J. has endured, and knows that her childhood innocence and ignorance about racism have been lost forever. Her final words are, "I cried for T. J. For T. J. and the land" (276).

Discussion

Roll of Thunder, Hear My Cry remains popular for many reasons. First, just as Pam Muñoz Ryan's *Esperanza Rising* provides a Latino perspective to life in the Great Depression, Taylor's novel shows how southern blacks lived during the 1930s. The Logans' story reveals the economic hardships endured by blacks in the Deep South during the Depression and shows how Jim Crow racism compounded their suffering. The novel also dispels many African American stereotypes. Cassie's family is unified, educated, and hardworking, and they are led by a strong father figure. Because they live in a society dominated by Jim Crow politics, the Logans are victims of racism, but their courage and unity give readers optimism that this family will not be crushed under the burden of white supremacy. *Roll of Thunder* is also an excellent example of historical fiction. Taylor weaves historical details from the 1930s with details from her own family history, and the book is an excellent model for students' own historical fiction. These qualities provide a springboard to classroom discussions about history, sociology, politics, and a wide variety of specific social issues that are still relevant today.

In addition to all of the above, *Roll of Thunder* is a text rich in the sorts of things English teachers admire: it's a good story well told. The story features a rich cast of interesting characters—heroes and villains—who are developed in a variety of ways. The central characters are complex and realistic; even the narrator, Cassie, has obvious flaws. Though it is longer than many young adult novels, the plot has plenty of tension and surprises that keep it from bogging down. The suspenseful plot holds readers' interest, and the genuine emotion readers derive from the characters' struggles elevates the book to something more than just a good historical novel. Taylor's artistry with words lifts the novel even higher. As the following sentence shows, she makes good use of figurative language and specific descriptive detail: "Before us the narrow, sun-splotched road wound like a lazy red serpent dividing the high forest bank of quiet, old trees on the left from the cotton field, forested by giant green and purple stalks on the right" (6). Though not cluttered by symbolism, *Roll of Thunder* does contain symbols for those who like to search for them. Perhaps the novel's most famous symbol is the fig tree on the Logans' property. Papa Logan points out that even though the bigger oak and walnut trees overshadow the fig, the smaller tree will survive because "that fig tree's got roots that run deep, and it belongs in that yard as much as the oak and walnut" (206). In addition to its aesthetic qualities, *Roll of Thunder* offers many opportunities to discuss thematic concerns of interest to teenagers: family, friendship, alienation, and equality.

Because *Roll of Thunder* is so popular, there is at least one reading guide, Laurie Rozakis' *A Reading Guide to Roll of Thunder, Hear My Cry*, and hundreds, perhaps thousands, of lesson plans available for teaching the novel. Many teachers have used the novel in literature circles; Rebecca Callan has even published *Literature Circle Guide: Roll of Thunder, Hear My Cry*. Janet Lopez, of Dzantik'i Heeni Middle School, in Juneau, Alaska, has developed guidelines for running literature circles that include *Roll of Thunder* (http://litsite.alaska.edu), and San Diego teacher Cheryl Ladley has designed a webquest using this novel. The book tends to be used in upper elementary and middle schools, though some high schools use it as well. *Roll of Thunder* often appears in English or language arts classes as part of a multicultural literature unit, but it is also effectively used during February's black history month and, of course, can be studied as a freestanding novel.

Prereading Questions and Writing Topics

(Also see the prereading activities in Appendix C.)

1. How does peer pressure affect your life? Your friends' lives? Have you ever done something you wish you hadn't because your peers were doing it?

2. Would you be willing to sacrifice something valuable in order to save a friend? Freewrite about a sacrifice you made in order to make life better for someone else.

3. What were "Jim Crow" laws? When did they originate? How were they enforced? If Jim Crow laws were applied to you now, what would you do?

4. The Great Depression (1929–1940) was a difficult era for all Americans. How was it even more difficult for African Americans?

5. Assume you are a farmer who owns his own land and whose family depends on the land and the crops it grows for survival. What would you do if people tried to steal your land?

6. What would you do if some loudmouthed, mean bullies told lies about your parents that resulted in your parents losing their jobs? And what if the loss of those jobs meant that you and your family might lose your home?

Questions for Writing and Discussion

1. Taylor describes rain this way: "the tat-tat of the rain against the tin roof changed to a deafening roar that sounded as if thousands of giant rocks

were being hurled against the earth" (45). Choose a sound occurring near where you live or go to school—falling rain, a train passing, a rushing river, cars honking, animals making sounds, etc.—and describe the sound in words.

2. After Big Ma tells Cassie that she must apologize to Lillian Jean Simms, Cassie can't understand why Big Ma didn't stick up for her. Stacey tells Cassie, "Well, maybe she couldn't help it, Cassie. Maybe she had to do it" (118). Why would Big Ma feel like she had to do this? Can you think of any examples from your life when an adult made you do something and you didn't understand why? Did you ever come to understand? Can you think of a situation in which an adult might ask a child to do something the child doesn't understand?

3. Reread Taylor's description of Cassie's feelings after the incident in Strawberry with Lillian Jean Simms: "A burning knot formed in my throat and I felt as if my body was not large enough to hold the frustration I felt, nor deep enough to drown the rising anger" (133). Think of a time in your life when you felt like this. Describe what was happening to make you feel this way. How did you manage your anger and frustration?

4. When Uncle Hammer discovers that Stacey gave away his new coat (given to Stacey as a gift by his uncle), Hammer says, "What the devil should he care what T. J. thinks or T. J. says? . . . I suppose if T. J. told you it was sum-mertime out there and you should run buck naked down the road because everybody else was doing it, you'd do that too, huh?" (142). Is Hammer too hard on Stacey? Is it always easy to stand up for yourself in the face of peer pressure? What kind of peer pressure have you faced? Were you able to make good decisions in the face of peer pressure?

5. When David Logan comes home for Christmas, Mr. Morrison, Hammer, Big Ma, and Mama sit around telling stories to their children, "acting out their tales with stageworthy skills, imitating the characters in voice, manner, and action so well that the listeners held their sides with laughter" (147). What important role does oral storytelling play in southern black culture? What role did storytelling play in Mildred D. Taylor's family (see the author's note at the beginning of the novel)? What role does storytelling play in your family?

6. Papa tells Stacey, "Maybe one day whites and blacks can be real friends, but right now the country ain't built that way" (158). Do you think the country is built that way now? Give evidence of how things have (or have not) changed since the 1930s.

7. Mama tells Mr. Granger that everything in the textbook isn't true. Do you think this is still true of textbooks today? If you have one, browse your history textbook. If you don't have one, borrow one. Do you think the book contains material that isn't true? Does it leave out information that is important and should be taught?

8. Look up information on church revivals. Is the one Mildred D. Taylor depicts in *Roll of Thunder* authentic? Is this something that would happen in every southern community? What was their role and purpose? Do they still happen today? What community events in your area bring people together?

9. The title of the novel comes from a song that Taylor created while she wrote the novel (the words appear at the beginning of Chapter 11). Why did Mildred D. Taylor choose this as the title? What meaning does the spiritual have? Research spirituals. When would this one have been sung? By whom?

10. What do you think would have happened to the Logan children if the bus driver, Ted Grimes, found out that they dug the ditch his bus eventually fell into? Were they right to be worried about night men?

Making Text-to-Text Connections to Other Stories

1. Uncle Hammer arrives at the Logan's home in a brand-new Packard. Compare the reaction to his purchase from his family members to the reaction that Wilbert gets from his family in *The Gold Cadillac*. How are the two situations similar? Different? Why are nice cars so important to Wilbert and to Hammer?

2. Cassie says to Stacey, "Ever since you went down into Louisiana to get Papa last summer you think you know so doggone much!" (118). The story of

Stacey going to Louisiana is told in *Song of the Trees*. How did this trip change Stacey? In what ways is he more grown up a year later?

3. Read Walter Dean Myers' *Monster* and compare Steve Harmon to T. J. Avery. In what ways did each bring trouble upon himself by seeking peer acceptance? How are they different? T. J.'s fate is much worse, in the end, than Steve's. Was it right that Steve didn't go to jail? Was it right that T. J. did? Did each get what he deserved?

4. After reading *Roll of Thunder, Hear My Cry*, consider the ending of *Song of the Trees.* Do you believe that David Logan would have dynamited his own trees to keep the lumbermen off his land? What evidence is there in *Roll of Thunder* that tells you that doing this would or would not be consistent with David's character?

5. Research the story of Emmett Till, a fourteen-year-old African American from Chicago who was murdered by white men in Mississippi in 1955. How is his case similar to T. J. Avery's? How are these stories different?

Additional Resources

Print Sources

Bosmajian, Hamida. 1996. "Mildred Taylor's Story of Cassie Logan: A Search for Law and Justice in a Racist Society." *Children's Literature* 24 (January): 141–60.

Brooks, Wanda, and Gregory Hampton. 2005. "Safe Discussions Rather Than Firsthand Encounters: Adolescents Examine Racism Through One Historical Text." *Children's Literature in Education* 36 (1) (March): 83–98.

Callan, Rebecca. 2003. *Literature Circle Guide: Roll of Thunder, Hear My Cry.* New York: Scholastic/Teaching Resources.

Faust, Mark A., and Nancy Glenzer. 2000. "'I could read those parts over and over': Eighth Graders Rereading to Enhance Enjoyment and Learning with Literature." *Journal of Adolescent and Adult Literacy* 44 (3) (November): 234–39.

Henderson, Laretta. 2005. "The Black Arts Movement and African American Young Adult Literature: An Evaluation of Narrative Style." *Children's Literature in Education* 36 (4) (December): 299–323.

Miller, Howard M. 1997. "Beyond 'Multicultural Moments.'" *English Journal* 86 (5) (September): 88–90.

Roll of Thunder, Hear My Cry. 2000. EMC Masterpiece Series. Access Edition. St. Paul, MN: EMC/Paradigm.

Rozakis, Laurie. 2003. *A Reading Guide to Roll of Thunder, Hear My Cry.* New York: Scholastic.

Sands, Barbara A. 1993. "Taking Time, Making Meaning: How Teachers and Students Make Meaning Using *Roll of Thunder, Hear My Cry.*" Diss. Madison: University of Wisconsin.

Stallworth, B. Joyce, Louel Gibbons, and Leigh Fauber. 2006. "It's Not on the List: An Exploration of Teachers' Perspectives on Using Multicultural Literature." *Journal of Adolescent & Adult Literacy* 46 (6) (March): 478–89.

Taylor, Mildred D. 1977. "Newbery Medal Acceptance Speech." *Horn Book Magazine* 53 (4) (August): 401-9.

Walker, Robbie Jean. 1990. "*Roll of Thunder, Hear My Cry.*" In *Beacham's Guide to Literature for Young Adults,* vol. 3, edited by Kirk H. Beetz, 1135–43. Washington, DC: Beacham.

Wehrmann, Kari Sue. 2000. "How to Differentiate Instruction: Baby Steps—A Beginner's Guide." *Educational Leadership* 58 (1) (September): 20–23. [Also found at www.nea.org/teachexperience/diffk021218.html.]

Wilhelm, Jeffrey D., Tanya Baker, and Julie Dube. 2001. *Strategic Reading: Guiding Students to Lifelong Literacy, K–12.* Portsmouth, NH: Heinemann.

Wormser, Richard. 2003. *The Rise and Fall of Jim Crow.* New York: St. Martin's.

Internet Sites

"African American Odyssey: The Depression, the New Deal, and World War II." http://lcweb2.loc.gov/ammem/aaohtml/exhibit/aopart8.html.

"America from the Great Depression to World War II." http://rs6.loc.gov/fsowhome.htm.

CyberGuide to *Roll of Thunder, Hear My Cry.* www.sdcoe.k12.ca.us/score/roll/rolltg.htm.

Davis School District Language Arts, "*Roll of Thunder, Hear My Cry.*" www.davis.k12.ut.us/curric/languagearts/grade8.html.

eMINTS National Center. Literature: *Roll of Thunder, Hear My Cry,* by Mildred D. Taylor. www.emints.org/ethemes/resources/S00001567.shtml.

"From Jim Crow to Linda Brown: A Retrospective of the African American Experience from 1897 to 1953." http://lcweb2.loc.gov/learn/lessons/97/crow/crowhome.html.

Internet School Library Media Center. Mildred Taylor Teacher Resource File. http://falcon.jmu.edu/~ramseyil/taylor.htm

The Learning Page/Lesson Plans. http://memory.loc.gov/learn/lessons/theme.html.

Literature Learning Ladders: *Roll of Thunder, Hear My Cry.* http://eduscapes.com/newbery/77a.html.

Lesson Plans for PBS's *The Rise and Fall of Jim Crow.* www.pbs.org/wnet/jimcrow/.

Roll of Thunder, Hear My Cry. http://faculty.salisbury.edu/~elbond/thunder.htm.

Web English Teacher. Mildred Taylor. Lesson Plans for *Roll of Thunder, Hear My Cry.* www.webenglishteacher.com/mtaylor.html.

Let the Circle Be Unbroken
The Politics of the Great Depression

 Synopsis

Taylor's third novel, *Let the Circle Be Unbroken* (1981), appeared as a sequel to *Roll of Thunder, Hear My Cry*, picking up where that novel left off: the trial of T. J. Avery. The story introduces many new characters, including members of the Logans' extended family, along with more historical detail than the previous two books. In addition to the oppression of Jim Crow culture, Franklin Delano Roosevelt's politics of the Great Depression provide additional conflict for the Logans and their neighbors. This novel won the Coretta Scott King Award and was named an ALA Notable Book and a Jane Addams Honor Book.

Setting
Rural Mississippi, 1934

Selected Characters

Cassie Logan, eleven years old

Papa, David Logan

Stacey Logan

Christopher-John Logan

Little Man, Clayton Chester Logan

Ma, Mary Louise Logan

Big Ma, Caroline Logan

Mr. L. T. Morrison

Uncle Hammer
T. J. Avery
Silas Lanier
Mrs. Lee Annie Lees
Clarice Wiggins
Wordell Lees
Little Willie Wiggins
Dubé Cross
Russell Thomas
Aunt Callie Jackson
Mr. Tom Bee
Mr. John Farnsworth
Mr. Wade Jamison
Joe McCalister
Clarence Hopkins
Moe Turner
Orris Turner
Elroy Turner
Judge Havershack
Jake Willis
Judge Forestor
Hadley Macabee
Mr. Deputy Haynes
Reverend Gabson

Mr. Tate Sutton
Mrs. Sutton
Jeremy Simms
R. W. Simms
Melvin Simms
Sheriff Hank Dobbs
Mr. Bastion Montier
Joe Billy Montier
Selma Montier
Harlan Granger
Mr. Henry Harrison
Stuart Walker
Pierceson Wells
Jacey Peters
Mr. Peters
Claude Avery
Mr. Hollenbeck
Morris Wheeler
John Moses
Cousin Bud Rankin
Suzella Rankin
Mr. Simms
Sheriff Conroy

Plot Summary

As a ten-year-old, Cassie Logan learned from firsthand experience that her world is filled with danger and injustice, and her education continues in *Let the Circle Be Unbroken*. The novel opens in 1934 and devotes most of its first three chapters to the trial of T. J. Avery, at which Cassie encounters a new kind of racism. In *Song of the Trees* and *Roll of Thunder, Hear My Cry*, the racism she most often experienced came from individuals who hated—or at least disrespected—her because she was black. At T. J.'s trial, however, she endures impersonal but equally painful institutional racism: segregated bathrooms and drinking fountains. Then she watches Mr. Jamison, a local lawyer and the Logans' advocate, work in vain as T. J.'s defense attorney. Even though he makes a diligent effort to present his client's case, he knows that the all-white jury decided the verdict before the trial even began. Despite Mr. Jamison's energetic defense and the overwhelming evidence that T. J. is innocent of murder, the jury returns with a guilty verdict and death sentence after deliberating for less than half an hour. Cassie is stunned by the glaring injustice.

In the fourth chapter, other plot lines begin to develop. Cassie learns about the complicated New Deal programs of President Franklin D. Roosevelt, programs designed to help poor farmers; unfortunately, in the South, the New Deal programs hurt more poor black farmers than they help. Morris Wheeler, a farmer's union representative, tries to organize the tenant farmers and sharecroppers in Great Faith, but his efforts are thwarted by the machinations of wealthy and influential landowners like Harlan Granger. The unsteady politics and economics of the Depression create tension for everyone, but when compounded by racism, the Depression threatens the security of the Logans and their black neighbors more than ever before. Because of the financial hardships at home, Stacey's friend Moe considers leaving the area to work for the Civilian Conservation Corps (CCC), one of the New Deal programs designed to create jobs for unemployed men. Amid the economic and political turmoil, Cassie begins to see that even the U.S. government seems bent on putting the Logan family and their land at peril.

Another subplot introduced in this chapter involves a friend of the Logan family, Mrs. Lee Annie Lees, who is determined to vote even though the impossibly difficult Jim Crow "literacy tests" are designed to prevent her and other blacks from registering. Mrs. Lee Annie Lees enlists Cassie's help in learning to read so she can memorize the state constitution, and this experience leads Cassie to discover yet another ugly reality of her world. As she herself learns about the Mississippi constitution, Cassie discovers that the white state government authorizes segregation and that white society is determined to prevent blacks from voting.

Cassie's coming of age escalates when she learns about an older black girl, Jacey Peters, and her flirtations with a white boy, Stuart Walker. When Cassie's family, especially Uncle Hammer, hear about Stuart and Jacey, they warn Cassie about white men's intentions toward black women, and this is Cassie's first encounter with Jim Crow sexuality. Her innocence erodes further with the appearance of her mother's cousin Bud Rankin, who confesses that he has married a white woman and is condemned by Uncle Hammer. Bud's mixed-race daughter, Suzella, lives with the Logans for a time, and her presence presents Cassie's parents and uncle many opportunities to explain to Cassie some of the complicated—and dangerous—issues of racism. Suzella is attractive to both young black and white men in the area, drawing special attention from Stacey's friend Russell Thomas, the smarmy outsider Jake Willis, and the wicked white boy Stuart Walker. Cassie learns the new facts of life when she understands that Jake's and Stuart's interest in Suzella is strictly sexual and that Stuart has gotten Jacey Peters pregnant. The racial tension created by the presence of Cousin Bud and Suzella also triggers Uncle Hammer's tirade against Stacey's and Cassie's friendship with Jeremy Simms. Hammer's initial outburst is followed by lectures from him and Papa about why blacks shouldn't befriend whites. These frank discussions go beyond the subtle initiatory talks Cassie's parents had with her about race in *Roll of Thunder, Hear My Cry*; now that Cassie is older, the issues have become more complex and more dangerous.

The failed economy of the Great Depression makes life difficult for everyone. Falling cotton prices and the generally poor economy mean that the Logans may not have the cash necessary to pay the taxes on their land. Harlan Granger makes several offers—and more than one underhanded attempt—to take over their land, but these threats only increase the Logans' resolve to save their property at all costs. Despite Ma's objections, Papa leaves home to resume his work on the railroad, and as family finances become even more dire, Stacey runs away with Moe Turner to work in cane fields in Louisiana. Stacey's determination to help the family leads him to join other desperately poor black men in the cane field work gangs. Though they'd been promised decent pay, the workers discover they have become captives of the field masters. Stacey's disappearance and the grave financial circumstances at home threaten to crack the rock-solid foundation of the Logan family.

The various subplots converge in the novel's final eighty pages. Cousin Bud is confronted by Stuart Walker and his goons, who harass him for "bedding" a white woman. As Cassie and Suzella watch in horror, Stuart humiliates Bud by ordering him to strip in front of the children. Dubé Cross tries to intervene, but he is roughed up by one of Stuart's pals. Only Mr. Morrison's timely arrival saves Bud and the children from what surely would have degenerated into a violent, tragic conclusion. Soon after this, Mrs. Lee Annie Lees goes into Strawberry to register to vote. Despite Cassie's tutoring and her own yearlong study, Mrs. Lee Annie Lees fails the literacy test, and Harlan Granger uses her violation of his orders not to register as an excuse to throw her and her sharecropping family off his land. At the same time, the political tensions in Strawberry boil over into a riot against the farmer's union. After the violence, the final plot complication—the Logans' fears for Stacey's safety—is resolved when, through the assistance of Mr. Jamison, the

Logans learn that Stacey is being held in a Louisiana jail. When they rescue him, the circle of the Logan family is whole once again.

 Discussion

The culture of the Great Depression influences all the conflicts in *Let the Circle Be Unbroken*. The unstable economy and the resulting poverty create fissures in the family when Papa and then Stacey leave home for work that promises needed cash. The falling cotton prices, the New Deal policies that limit planting, and the economic desperation, all of which foster a desire for union protection, compound the problems the Logans face. The harsh economic conditions exacerbate racial tensions; sharecropping white farmers resent landowning black farmers, white landowners are more determined than ever to maintain their hold on their share-croppers and tenant farmers, and poor whites turn their anger and frustration on blacks and union organizers.

By the end of the novel, Cassie has learned some of the seamier and more violent aspects of racism, but she is not the only character to have learned hard lessons about life. All the Logan children believe that Mr. Jamison and the American legal system will save T. J. from a death sentence, but their hopes are dashed when they watch the all-white jury condemn T. J. to death for a murder he didn't commit. The trial's conclusion is painful evidence to the Logan children that the U.S. legal system does not protect black Americans. Suzella learns that look-ing white isn't the same as being white. Stacey's experience in the cane fields teaches him that he can't believe everything he hears and that being young, strong, and courageous is no protection against exploitation by the white majori-ty. Papa learns that his family needs him at home more than it needs his income from working for the railroad. Mrs. Lee Annie Lees discovers that her best patri-otic desire and most diligent efforts can't overcome the Jim Crow barriers to vot-ing. The failure of the farmer's union teaches Dubé Cross that even the noblest ideas wilt under the pressures of poverty, fear, and greed.

Of course, as the narrator and protagonist, Cassie's education is most poignant. In *Roll of Thunder*, she was introduced to a few of the realities of the racist South, but in *Let the Circle Be Unbroken*, the realities are harsher, more painful, and more pervasive than she has previously known. Once again, her family and her natural intelligence and courage prevent her from being consumed by the maelstrom of problems whirling around her, but by the end of the novel Cassie is no longer the naive, innocent girl she was in *Song of the Trees* or *Roll of Thunder*.

Because American history is more prominent in *Let the Circle Be Unbroken* than in Taylor's previous stories, the novel presents teachers and students with many opportunities to discuss the historical facts of the Great Depression and the United States' efforts to overcome economic disaster. Readers also have an opportunity to experience, vicariously, the deprivations many Americans experienced in the 1930s. In addition to understanding better the economic hardships of the Depression, readers will gain insight into the Jim Crow culture of Mississippi at the time and see how institutional racism subjugated and injured thousands of people during a time when they were already enduring unimaginable poverty.

The New Deal policies and political movements like the Southern Tenant Farmers Union are important aspects of this novel, but so are a racism and segregation similar to that which Taylor herself experienced and read about during her childhood in the 1950s. Taylor was twelve years old when the grotesque photograph of the mutilated corpse of fourteen-year-old Emmett Till appeared in *Jet Magazine* and when the trial of his white killers ended with an acquittal from an all-white Mississippi jury. The trial was widely covered in the black media and bears many similarities to the fictional murder trial of T. J. Avery. A historical figure may also have been the basis for one of Taylor's *Let the Circle Be Unbroken* subplots. Prior to the passage of various Civil Rights Acts in the 1960s, nearly all black citizens in Mississippi were barred from registering to vote. The efforts of Mrs. Lee Annie Lees to register are similar to the famous activist Fannie Lou Hamer's attempts to vote. In 1962, Hamer and her husband were thrown off the Mississippi plantation they sharecropped because she tried to register to vote. The fictional characters and events in *Let the Circle Be Unbroken* that are based on real people and events offer students a chance to probe details of American history that may be absent from or underrepresented in their history textbooks.

Though *Let the Circle Be Unbroken* is clearly a sequel to *Roll of Thunder, Hear My Cry* and though it maintains the same setting and many of the same characters that appear in Taylor's first two books, the book does not turn the Logan stories into a series. Each book in the Logan family saga is a sequel (or a prequel), but the stories are distinct enough to stand alone. More important, *Let the Circle Be Unbroken*'s main character experiences real growth. Cassie at the conclusion of the novel is not the same girl she was at the beginning. Of course she is a year older, but she's many years wiser after experiencing the various conflicts and characters that the novel comprises.

Prereading Questions and Writing Topics

(Also see the prereading activities in Appendix C.)

1. Read the April 28, 2005, article entitled "All In," which can be found on sportsillustrated.com (http://sportsillustrated.cnn.com/2005/sioncampus/04/25/poker0428/index.html). You may also want to read the accompanying articles in their special report about Internet poker and online gambling. You could also research more about the online gambling craze from other sources. Do you think that gambling is a problem for people your age? Do you know anyone at your school who gambles over the Internet? Do you do so yourself?

2. Consider the jury system of trials in the United States. Is a jury of peers a fair body for determining justice? Can you think of any trials where a jury made a wrong decision based on something other than the facts in the case? For example, in the trials of celebrities O. J. Simpson and Michael Jackson, were the jurors swayed by the defendants' celebrity status? You could watch the film *Twelve Angry Men* to get an idea of how juries work.

3. Research the Civilian Conservation Corps (CCC) and the Works Progress Administration (WPA). How did these government programs help people during the Depression? Who, if anyone, did they hurt?

4. Though the United States is a democracy, it wasn't until well into the twentieth century that all citizens enjoyed the right to vote. Who has been denied the right to vote in the past? Why? Who was Fannie Lou Hamer? Why is she an important figure in the history of civil rights?

5. What do you know about unions? What are some of the goals of labor unions? Who do they protect? Who or what might oppose unions? Why?

6. Read the trial scenes from the novels *To Kill a Mockingbird or Mississippi Trial, 1955* or the nonfiction book *Getting Away with Murder: The True Story*

of the Emmett Till Case. How did Jim Crow laws and racist attitudes affect the outcomes of the trials presented in these books? How might racial attitudes affect a trial today?

7. Imagine that you're a strong and capable teenager in a very poor farming family. Your family has never had much money, but a run of bad weather and bad luck has made this year particularly bleak. The family is in a desperate situation, and if they don't get money soon, they'll lose their home and their farm. You hear about a risky but well-paying job in another state. Your parents have told you not to consider this job, but you know that the money you could earn would solve all your family's financial problems. What will you do?

Questions for Writing and Discussion

1. Cassie says, "Maybe it was the way of life to change, but if I had my way I would put an iron padlock on time so nothing would ever have to change again" (13). If you could put an "iron padlock" on time, would you? And if so, at what age would you do so? Why doesn't Cassie want things to change?

2. Do you agree with Papa that playing marbles can escalate into gambling and should be avoided? Do you know anyone who gambles regularly? Has he or she lost a lot of money? Why does Papa want to make sure his children don't get into gambling?

3. Cassie explains the Turners' sharecropping situation: as sharecroppers they were tied to the land for as long as Mr. Montier wanted them there. Mr. Montier provided everything for them—their land, their mule, their plow, their seed—in return for a portion of their cotton. When they needed food or other supplies, they bought on credit at a store approved by Mr. Montier where high interest rates upped the price tremendously on everything they bought. At year's end, when all the cotton had been sold and the accounts were figured by Mr. Montier, the Turners were usually in more debt than they had been at the beginning of the year. And as long as they were in debt, they could not just up and leave the land on their own, not unless

they wanted the sheriff after them (89–90). Research sharecropping. Is this situation typical of all sharecroppers? Do you think this is a fair system? Is there still sharecropping today? If not, when and why did it end?

4. In concluding her description of the trial, Cassie says, "There was to be no mercy" (85). Why did Taylor have Cassie use the word *mercy*? Shouldn't it be *justice*? If T. J. was innocent of the murder, which he was, he didn't need mercy, he needed justice. Is the jury system a fair way to decide criminal cases?

5. Consider the children who study with Ma on weekends and Moe Turner, who walks three and a half miles each way to school every day. Also, consider Lee Annie, Big Ma, and Tom Bee, who want to learn about the state constitution. Why is education so important to these people? Why are they willing to make sacrifices to attend school? Are you willing to make these same kinds of sacrifices to be able to attend school? Does these characters' behavior change the way you feel about an education?

6. Why would Suzella's passing for white be so dangerous for her and for the Logans?

7. Research scarlet fever. What is it? Does it still exist today? How did people die from it?

8. The Logans sing "Will the Circle Be Unbroken." The title of the book obviously comes from this spiritual. Find the lyrics of this song, then explain why you think Taylor chose this as her novel's title. What is it about the song that matches up with the events of the novel?

9. Harlan Granger plays an important role in this story. How would some of the novel's conflicts have been resolved differently if Harlan Granger were a friend to the Logans instead of an enemy?

10. What effect does the subplot of Mrs. Lee Annie Lees and her efforts to vote have on the novel as a whole? When did the United States government finally pass laws to protect the voting rights of all citizens? How effective were those laws?

Making Text-to-Text Connections to Other Stories

1. Compare and contrast Stacey's experience in the cane fields in *Let the Circle Be Unbroken* with Paul-Edward Logan's experience in logging camps in *The Land*. Explain how each experience influences the characters and the plots of the respective novels.

2. Taylor is often praised for her use of strong female characters. Cassie, of course, is one. Make a list of other strong female characters in the Logan stories and make a list of their strengths. Then highlight characteristics that all the girls and women have in common.

3. As he did in *Roll of Thunder*, Uncle Hammer arrives at the Logans' home in a car. At church, there is a lot of discussion about this car compared with his Packard. Compare the reaction to this car with the reaction to the Packard. Why does it matter so much to the blacks who live near the Logans that Uncle Hammer drives a car? Why was the time he arrived in the Packard a monumental event for them?

4. Bud Rankin and Suzella appear for the first time in this novel. Identify other new or nonrecurring characters in other Logan stories and compare their roles to the roles of Bud and Suzella.

5. Read Harper Lee's *To Kill a Mockingbird* and Chris Crowe's *Mississippi Trial, 1955*. Each of these novels includes a trial similar to the one in *Let the Circle Be Unbroken*. Compare and contrast the three trials. What is similar/different about the cases? What racial attitudes affected these trials?

Additional Resources

Print Resources

Bosmajian, Hamida. 1996. "Mildred Taylor's Story of Cassie Logan: A Search for Law and Justice in a Racist Society." *Children's Literature* 24 (January): 141–60.

Chura, Patrick. 2000. "Prolepsis and Anachronism: Emmett Till and the Historicity of *To Kill a Mockingbird*." *Southern Literary Journal* 32 (2) (Spring): 1–26.

Piper, Adrian. 1992. "Passing for White, Passing for Black." *Transition* 58: 4–32.

Wormser, Richard. 2003. *The Rise and Fall of Jim Crow*. New York: St. Martin's.

Internet Sites

"African American Odyssey: The Depression, the New Deal, and World War II." http://memory.loc.gov/ammem/aaohtml/exhibit/aopart8.html.

"America from the Great Depression to World War II: Photographs from the FSA-OWI, 1935–1945." http://memory.loc.gov/ammem/fsowhome.html.

"Case in Point: Learning About the Significance of Court Cases in the History of Civil Rights." New York Times Learning Network. www.nytimes.com /learning/teachers/lessons/20040514friday.html?searchpv=learning_lessons.

A Guide to *Let the Circle Be Unbroken*. http://eolit.hrw.com/hlla/novelguides/hs /Mini-Guide.Taylor.pdf.

The Learning Page/Lesson Plans. http://memory.loc.gov/learn/lessons/theme .html.

The Rise and Fall of Jim Crow. PBS. www.pbs.org/wnet/jimcrow/.

The Road to Memphis
World War II and the Winds of Change

Synopsis

Published in 1990, the same year as *Mississippi Bridge*, *The Road to Memphis* continues the Logan family saga with a more mature Cassie narrating the story. Critic Joel Chaston distinguishes this novel from Taylor's other books as "bleaker than some of the earlier Logan stories. . . . *The Road to Memphis* is itself an important book because it lets readers see characters from Taylor's earlier books as they are on the verge of becoming adults. Cassie and Stacey are no longer able to hide behind their father, David Logan, and go on a journey during which they must confront racial hatred directly" (3891). In addition to being named a Notable Book and a Best Book for Young Adults by the American Library Association, the novel won the 1991 Coretta Scott King Award.

Setting
Mississippi, 1941

Characters

Christopher-John, fifteen

Little Man, fourteen

Cassie, seventeen

Stacey, twenty

Jeremy Simms, twenty
Statler Aames, Jeremy's cousin
Troy Aames, Jeremy's cousin
Leon Aames, Jeremy's cousin
Harris Mitchum
Sissy Mitchum, Harris' twin
Moe Turner
Little Willie Wiggins
Clarence Hopkins
Kaleb Wallace
Mr. Wade Jamison
Mama, Mary Logan
Big Ma, Caroline Logan
Papa, David Logan
Charlie Simms
Joe Billy Montier
Uncle Hammer

Mr. Turner
Reverend Gabson
J. D. Hopkins
Mr. Harlan Granger
Mr. Farnsworth
Cousin Hugh Reams, Big Ma's sister's son
Sylvie Reams
Oliver Reams
Mrs. Mabel Stalnaker
Sheriff Hank Dobbs
Deputy Haynes
Solomon Bradley
Mag
Aunt Hannah Mays
Ma Dessie
Mort Jones

Plot Summary

Cassie, now seventeen, lives in Jackson where she attends high school. The novel opens with Cassie, who is visiting her family, sitting in the family wagon with her younger brothers across from the Wallace store, waiting for Stacey's bus from Jackson, where he now lives as well. As it has been in most of Taylor's previous novels, the Wallace store continues to be the hub of trouble. When one of the Logans' friends, Harris Mitchum, heads into the store, Cassie decides to join him despite Christopher-John's warning: "Every time we set foot in there, Cassie, there's trouble, and we don't need any more trouble" (9). His warning foreshadows the conflict that will be the catalyst for the main action in the rest of the novel.

The three Aames brothers, Jeremy Simms's cousins, harass Harris in the store and don't stop until Jeremy intervenes. Harris leaves the store, humiliated, and joins the Logans to wait for Stacey. When the bus arrives without Stacey and his two friends, Moe Turner and Little Willie Wiggins, who work with him in a box factory in Jackson, the Logan children decide to head home. On their way, they encounter a shiny new car, driven by Stacey. While his siblings admire his new purchase, Stacey explains that he bought the car from the local lawyer, Mr. Wade Jamison. The car provides the setting for two important scenes: later that day Moe confesses his affection for Cassie, and when Jeremy Simms comes to the Logan home to see the new car, he expresses his appreciation for his longtime, though distant, friendship with Stacey.

The nostalgic feelings from these scenes of friendship evaporate quickly when Stacey, Cassie, and their friends go coon hunting. While Cassie and Harris are tracking in the woods, they meet Jeremy and the Aames brothers, who, after threatening Cassie and Harris, decide to make Harris their prey in the hunt. Jeremy tries to prevent the abuse, but Statler Aames shames him into joining the chase. Cassie finds Stacey and the other boys and tells them what has happened, and they finally find Harris, treed by the Aameses and their dogs. As tensions escalate, the tree branch holding Harris snaps and he crashes to the ground, knocking himself unconscious and shattering his leg. The accident makes the Aameses back off, and when Jeremy asks if he can help with Harris, Stacey turns on him: "You were hunting Harris down. I don't expect so" (71).

With the help of Big Ma, the Logans and their friends load Harris onto a wagon and take him to the Logan home where he can be tended to. Later, Jeremy shows up, penitent and concerned about Harris. Blaming him for what happened to her twin brother, Sissy Mitchum nearly attacks Jeremy but is restrained by her boyfriend, Clarence Hopkins. Papa sends Stacey out to talk to Jeremy, and Stacey refuses to accept Jeremy's apology, explanation, or friendship. "You hunted Harris down. That's all I know . . . or need to know" (78). After watching the scene and Jeremy's sad departure from the Logan home, Cassie concludes the chapter with, "I looked out to the woods and figured maybe it was just as well that this had happened. After all, Jeremy was a man now, and childhood was over. Appropriately, I supposed, so was our friendship" (78).

Stacey, Moe, and Little Willie return to Jackson with Cassie, and the week after Thanksgiving, they're called home to attend the funeral of Reverend Gabson, longtime pastor of the Great Faith Church. Immediately on their return to Strawberry, the story becomes more complicated. Clarence's girlfriend, Sissy, is pregnant, and though the boys know that Clarence in the father, Sissy claims it could be any one of the boys, including Stacey. She confesses to Cassie that her story is a plot to get Clarence to declare his love for her and to assume responsibility for his child; Cassie thinks the idea, and Sissy, is crazy. As Cassie is walking back to the church from Sissy's home, she's stopped by the three Aames brothers, and Statler Aames threatens to rape her but is prevented when Papa suddenly shows up. In the background of this action is talk of war, jobs, and the future.

Stacey's hoping for a job in a trucking firm; Moe is talking about enlisting in the military like Clarence has done. Moe hopes to earn enough money to purchase land of his own, land that he can one day share with Cassie. Cassie just wants to go to college.

Stacey, Cassie, and their friends stop in Strawberry on their way back to Jackson so Stacey can make his final car payment to Mr. Jamison; while in town, he also decides to change one of his car's tires. The Aames brothers are hanging around, and one of them baits Clarence, then tries to force him to let an old white man rub his head for "good luck." Though she hates what the brothers are doing to Clarence, Cassie is helpless to prevent it. Moe tries to intervene and the Aames boys resent his interference, but before they can attack him, Mr. Jamison breaks things up. Not long after, when the car is in the garage getting its tire changed, the Aames brothers show up and immediately begin taunting Moe. When Statler makes a sexual comment about Cassie, Moe snaps, severely beating all three brothers with a tire iron. Jeremy hides Moe under a tarp in his father's truck just seconds before a crowd of angry white men come on the scene, ready to lynch Moe and anyone else involved in the beating. While the sheriff and the other white men are out of sight, Stacey convinces Jeremy to smuggle Moe out of Strawberry and take him to Jackson. Despite knowing full well what might happen to him if his father finds out what he's done, Jeremy agrees.

Little Willie, Clarence, Stacey, and Cassie return to Jackson but can't find Moe. While they're trying to determine where Moe is, Cassie has a chance meeting with a young black lawyer from Memphis, Solomon Bradley, who simultaneously flirts with her and encourages her dream of going to law school. Later, Moe returns. The trip had taken longer than expected, Jeremy explains, because he had to take a load of goods to another town, and the truck had broken down along the way. Unsure of what to do next, the friends consult with Mr. Jamison at his Jackson office, and he advises them that the best thing to do is to get Moe up north. In the meantime, they learn that men in Strawberry assume that someone smuggled Moe out of town. They suspect Mr. Jamison, but he is cleared. Now they're looking for Stacey and his friends. The young people decide they must head to Memphis immediately.

On the way to Memphis, Stacey, Cassie, and their three friends have several close encounters and terrifying escapes—compounded by their concern about Clarence's increasingly severe headaches. When it's clear that Clarence is seriously ill, they try to check him into a white hospital; they're rejected, of course, and end up placing him with a local black woman, a healer, before they continue to Memphis. They go straight to the train station, planning to buy Moe a ticket to Chicago where he'll be met by Uncle Hammer. The station is unusually crowded, and they're unable to buy a ticket because the Japanese have just attacked Pearl Harbor and servicemen have priority on all trains leaving Memphis.

The next-to-last chapter is titled "The Memphis Prince," and the title suggests how Cassie regards the handsome Solomon Bradley, whom they seek out for help when they can't purchase a ticket for Moe. Solomon provides refuge for the four young people and uses his connections to acquire a ticket to Chicago. Cassie is smitten with Solomon, charmed by his good looks, sharp mind, and successful life. Cassie's affection for Solomon Bradley complicates her relationship with Moe, and when Cassie tries to explain and to apologize, Moe stops her. "Cassie, I told you, you don't never have to explain nothing to me. Never" (254). Cassie, Little Willie, and Stacey take Moe to the station, where Moe says goodbye to Cassie and confesses his love for her. After seeing Moe off, the three friends return to the old woman's house where they had left Clarence but discover that he has died from a cerebral hemorrhage. Cassie describes her reaction to the news this way: "The night blackened and nothing was the same" (262).

The last chapter, "A Final Farewell," is laden with sadness and farewells. Cassie and Stacey go back to Strawberry to break the news about Clarence's death. When they arrive in town, the sheriff and other white men, believing that Harris helped Moe escape, are holding Harris captive. Sissy is hysterical, and when the Simms' pickup pulls up, she launches into wild accusations that Jeremy Simms is the one who smuggled Moe out of town. When Jeremy confesses, his father erupts, giving him a brutal beating in front of the gathered crowd. In the most heart-wrenching scene of all of Taylor's stories, Jeremy pleads to his father, but Charlie turns on his son with inhuman hatred: "Don't you never again let me see you in this life, boy. Can't stand the sight of ya" (275). Sheriff Dobbs intervenes, asking Charlie to take Jeremy home so his mother can tend to his injuries, but once again, Charlie Simms shows himself to be irredeemably evil by refusing to care for his son. "Far's I'm concerned, he's got no ma, no pa either. He got no family now. . . . He dead t' me" (276).

From this awful scene, the story moves on to Sissy who, on hearing that Clarence is dead, refuses to believe Cassie and Stacey. In a fit of madness, she clings to the story that Clarence will be home for Christmas and that they'll be married. Harris takes her aside to comfort her, and as Cassie and Stacey leave they hear Sissy "scream Clarence's name, and her scream was like a knife that rent the afternoon asunder" (280). The town holds a wake and then a funeral for Clarence, and after the funeral the Logans gather at home and, with the pall of war hanging over them, talk about the future. Christopher-John and Little Man want to enlist as soon as they're old enough, and it's assumed that Stacey will soon be drafted. Amid the sadness and uncertainty, Papa calls the family together to pray. Not long after the prayer, Jeremy appears at the doorstep to say goodbye before he goes to Jackson to join the Army. In a final poignant scene, Jeremy thanks the Logan children for their friendship and asks them to remember him after he's gone. The novel concludes with these simple lines:

> The night passed.
> The morning came.
> Stacey left.
> We did not see Jeremy Simms again. (290)

Discussion

Chaston's characterization of *The Road to Memphis* is right on target; this is the bleakest of all Taylor's stories. Cassie, at seventeen, is now mature enough and experienced enough to see her Mississippi world for what it is: a dangerous, racist place, heading into world war. Because she is older and wiser in this novel, she is more independent than ever. Her family and family values still provide a secure foundation, but she has moved away from that foundation literally and emotionally. On the road to Memphis, she encounters vile, cruel racism unblunted by any family intervention. She faces love and death and war all in the space of a few days, and she knows that neither she nor her world will ever be the same. The winds of change that started in Pearl Harbor have caught up with her in Mississippi, and when she returns from Memphis, she reports:

> Before noon we were back in Strawberry. Nothing had changed in the town during our few short days away, though I supposed, because so much in our lives had changed, that it would be changed too. . . . The forest, the fields, everything was the same as before we had left, and that seemed strange to me, for our lives had changed so that they would never be the same again. (267)

At the conclusion of *The Road to Memphis*, Cassie has completed her own road to adulthood; the coming-of-age process that began in *Song of the Trees* ends in this novel with Cassie on the brink of independence, contemplating love, career, and the fate of the world. She is no longer naive about any aspect of racism, and she is more determined than ever to overcome the bonds of Jim Crow.

Fans of Mildred D. Taylor's books may be surprised by the darker, harsher tone that permeates *The Road to Memphis*. Indeed, the painful scenes in the novel stack up like cars in a train wreck: Harris is taunted by racists, then abused by them during a coon hunt; Reverend Gabson dies; Sissy Harris is pregnant but unmarried; Cassie narrowly escapes being raped; racist taunting makes Moe snap, beat his tormentors, and then run for his life; Cassie is almost beaten for using a whites-only bathroom; Stacey, Cassie, Clarence, and Moe drive back roads to avoid being captured by a lynch mob; the Japanese attack Pearl Harbor and war breaks out; Moe flees to Chicago to save his life; Clarence dies because he's denied admission to a white hospital; Jeremy Simms is beaten and disowned by his father; Stacey may soon be drafted to fight in the war. Cassie faces all of these painful events head on and personally, and because she does, so do Taylor's readers. Unlike Taylor's previous novels, *The Road to Memphis* has few scenes of nostalgic warmth or comfort. Papa and Mama aren't around to mute the pain or to put it into a context that helps Cassie understand. The absence of those tender or comforting scenes lets readers feel the burden Cassie feels.

The novel's tragic and painful plot is not the only reason *The Road to Memphis* is harsher than the rest of the Logan saga. Cassie's narration contributes to the more bitter tone. She's begun to weary of the racist obstacles she's faced most of her life. The suffering of her family and friends, the ubiquitous segregation, and the racist hatred frustrate and anger her. She's old enough now to look ahead in life, but it's difficult for Cassie to be optimistic about her future when everything is so uncertain. America's involvement in World War II will certainly affect her life, but so will Jim Crow. If Cassie doesn't already know it, Solomon Bradley has affirmed that she is a bright young woman loaded with potential, but by the end of *The Road to Memphis*, she sees a future that will be, at best, bittersweet:

> I didn't know much of anything about this war we were in. . . . All I knew was that people who had always been a part of my life, people I loved—and that included Jeremy Simms—were leaving, and some were not coming back. All I knew was that my brother would be leaving, too, and that I was fearful of what was to come. (288)

Cassie knows that neither she nor the world of her childhood will ever be the same, and, like many of Taylor's young adult readers, she is uncertain about and perhaps even afraid of what the future will bring.

Classroom discussions about *The Road to Memphis* can easily focus on its place in the Logan family saga and how it is similar to and different from Taylor's other books. Students might also consider why this novel's tone differs so much from Taylor's other books. The age and maturity of the narrator is one explanation, but the historical setting may be another. Mildred D. Taylor was born in Mississippi in 1943, not quite two years after the attack on Pearl Harbor, and even though she was raised in Ohio, she visited Mississippi often enough to see the "White Only" signs of segregation in the South and to experience the fear that racism imposes on its victims. In other words, unlike all her previous books—with the exception of *The Gold Cadillac*—*The Road to Memphis* depends more on Taylor's own experience and less on family stories. The suffering Cassie endures and the frustration she feels from the various events in the novel have some basis in Taylor family stories, but it is likely that they also are strongly rooted in Taylor's personal experience.

At the time of this writing, Taylor's promised final novel of the Logan family saga, tentatively titled *Logan*, has not yet been published; that leaves *The Road to Memphis* as the last of the Logan stories. Reading this novel offers students many opportunities to speculate about how the Logan stories—how Cassie's story—will ultimately conclude. *The Road to Memphis* leaves Cassie on the brink of adulthood with several unresolved plot questions: What will happen to Moe? Will Moe and Cassie get together? What will Cassie do after high school? What will happen to Stacey? What will happen to Sissy and her baby? Will Solomon Bradley cross Cassie's path again? These questions and others like them provide opportunities for students to practice prediction strategies and will most likely lead to interesting class discussions and writing assignments about the Logan family and their stories as told in the nine books Mildred D. Taylor has published so far.

Prereading Questions and Writing Topics

(Also see the prereading Activities in Appendix C.)

1. Is it sometimes necessary to lie? If so, think of a situation in which lying

would be not only ethical but necessary. Have you ever been in such a situation?

2. Have you or a friend had a family member or someone close to you die unexpectedly? What effects did the death have on family members and friends? What did family members and friends do to cope with the loss and move on with life?

3. Imagine that you're a teenager in December 1941 and you've just heard about the attack on Pearl Harbor. Soon the United States will enter World War II. How will the war change your life and the lives of your family and friends?

4. Have you ever been on a long road trip (by car, bus, or train)? Remember your trip and write about memorable events. Did you have any adventures along the way? Did you stop at any unique towns? Did you meet any interesting people?

5. Research the role of the Supreme Court in the United States. What kinds of cases does the Court hear? What kind of power does the Court have? How many justices sit on the Court? How are cases argued?

6. While you're watching, one of your best friends is attacked by a dangerous gang member; in self-defense, your friend accidentally kills the gang member. Minutes after the fight, other members of the gang hear about what happened and come searching for your friend, threatening to kill him as soon as they find him. What's the right thing to do? What's the wise thing to do? What would you do in this situation?

Questions for Writing and Discussion

1. Who are the tragic characters in this novel? How does their tragic suffering affect Cassie? How does it affect the story?

2. Research the role of African American soldiers in World War II. *The Road to Memphis* has black characters who are excited about the opportunity to serve their country and fight in the war and black characters who feel it's a

white man's war. What percentage of American troops in World War II were African American? Did these soldiers hold leadership positions? How were they treated when they returned?

3. Solomon Bradley asks Cassie Logan about *Plessy v. Ferguson*, the Supreme Court ruling that found racial segregation Constitutional, so long as it was "separate but equal." Research this Supreme Court decision and its aftermath. How long was segregation legal? What changed to make it illegal? Why did the Supreme Court originally rule for the Constitutionality of segregation?

4. When Mag, the woman who works on Solomon Bradley's newspaper, says goodbye to Cassie, she hugs her and whispers, "Now, you take care, girl, and don't you be thinking on Solomon. You forget about him. He's too much for you" (255). Do you think Cassie should stop thinking about Solomon? What might happen to her if she pursues her feelings for him? Why does Mag give this advice? Is it good advice?

5. Do you think Clarence and Sissy act responsibly about their child-to-be? Are they each ready to be parents? What challenges might they have faced if Clarence had lived and they had gotten married?

6. Two characters who have played important roles throughout the Logan family novels die in this novel—Reverend Gabson and Clarence Hopkins. Compare and contrast the community reaction to these two deaths. Why is the reaction so different? Why is one seen as much more tragic than the other, though both are from natural causes?

7. Predict what will happen to Jeremy Simms. Do you think he will ever reconcile with his father? Will he fight in the war? What will happen to him after the war? Where will he live? What will he do in life?

8. Why does Jeremy Simms refuse to help Harris get out of the hunt initiated by Jeremy's cousins? Did he deserve the treatment he received from Stacey?

9. Because of choices they made, two members of the community likely can never return to their hometown again—Moe and Jeremy. Compare and contrast the choices these two characters made. Were they worth the conse-

quences? Were they noble choices? Moral ones? Immoral? Wrong? Right? What would you have done in their situations?

10. What do you think will happen to Cassie Logan? Will she become a lawyer? Will she remain in Mississippi? Will she marry or remain single? Justify your predictions.

 ## Making Text-to-Text Connections to Other Stories

1. In *The Road to Memphis*, Charlie Simms' truck runs off the road to avoid Stacey's new car. How is that similar to a scene in *The Well* when David and Hammer Logan encounter Charlie Simms when his wagon is stuck in a ditch? Find other roadside encounters in *The Gold Cadillac, Roll of Thunder, Hear My Cry,* and other Logan stories. What do the readers learn from these encounters?

2. Stacey's car plays an important role in *The Road to Memphis*. In both *Roll of Thunder* and *Let the Circle Be Unbroken*, Uncle Hammer arrives in a car. Compare the reaction to Hammer's purchases from his family members to the reaction that Wilbert gets from his family in *The Gold Cadillac* and Stacey gets in *The Road to Memphis*. How are these situations similar? Different? Why do cars matter so much to Wilbert? To Hammer? To Stacey?

3. In this novel, Jeremy Simms risks his life to save Moe's. In what ways has Jeremy defied his father and the expectations of white society in the other Logan family novels? How has he suffered for his choices? Why is he willing to do this?

4. Compare and contrast the character of Cassie Logan in *Roll of Thunder, Hear My Cry* with Cassie Logan in *The Road to Memphis*. Pay particular attention to how she has matured and to which character traits she retains, even into her teenage years.

5. Explain how U.S. history plays different roles in the plots of *The Road to Memphis, The Land,* and *Roll of Thunder, Hear My Cry.*

6. Taylor has said that she will write one more book in the Logan family saga. Predict what might happen to various characters—for example, Stacey Logan, Jeremy Simms, Solomon Bradley, Moe Turner, and Cassie Logan—in this final book. Where do you think the family will end up?

7. What is the history of the Logan land in Taylor's novels? What was Paul-Edward Logan's role in acquiring the land? Who consistently worked to take the land from the Logans? What are some things the Logans did to keep their land? To get started, take a look at these pages: *Roll of Thunder, Hear My Cry*, 6–8, 90–95, 168–70; *Let the Circle Be Unbroken*, 128–30; *The Land*, 160–61, 339–60.

8. In most of the Logan stories, fathers talk to their children about "using your head": "You clear your head so you can think sensibly" (*Roll of Thunder, Hear My Cry*, 176); "Don't get so smart, Daughter, you don't use your head" (*Road to Memphis*, 105); "You boys better start learning how to use your heads, not your fists" (*The Well*, 72); "Then you use what you're strongest at, boy! You use your head" (*The Land*, 5). How do the Logan children use their heads to solve their problems? What happens when they don't use their heads?

9. In her Newbery Award acceptance speech, Taylor said that one of her goals was to "paint a truer picture of black people. I wanted to show the endurance of the black world, with strong fathers and concerned mothers; I wanted to show happy, loved children about whom other children, both black and white, could say, 'Hey, I really like them! I feel what they feel.' I wanted to show a black family united in love and pride, of which the reader would like to be a part." Consider the Logan stories and whether or not Taylor achieved her goals.

10. Make a timeline of the important characters and events in the nine Logan stories and then consider these questions: What characters has Taylor sustained throughout the Logan saga? Why has she kept them in the stories? Which characters appear in only one book? Why? Do any historical gaps exist? If so, where?

Additional Resources

Print Sources

Bosmajian, Hamida. 1996. "Mildred Taylor's Story of Cassie Logan: A Search for Law and Justice in a Racist Society." *Children's Literature* 24 (January): 141–60.

Chaston, Joel. 1994. "*The Road to Memphis.*" In *Beacham's Guide to Literature for Young Adults*, vol. 8, edited by Kirk H. Beetz, 3890–97. Washington, DC: Beacham.

Henderson, Laretta. 2005. "The Black Arts Movement and African American Young Adult Literature: An Evaluation of Narrative Style." *Children's Literature in Education* 36 (4) (December): 299–323.

Schneider, Dean. 2004. "Mississippi 1941: A Perilous Journey." *Book Links* 13 (3) (January): 35–38.

Taylor, Mildred D. 1977. "Newbery Medal Acceptance Speech." *Horn Book Magazine* 53 (4) (August): 401–9.

Wormser, Richard. 2003. *The Rise and Fall of Jim Crow*. New York: St. Martin's.

Internet Sites

"African American Odyssey: The Depression, the New Deal, and World War II." http://lcweb2.loc.gov/ammem/aaohtml/exhibit/aopart8.html.

"America from the Great Depression to World War II." http://memory.loc.gov .ammem/fsowhome.htm.

The Learning Page/Lesson Plans. http://memory.loc.gov/learn/lessons/theme .html.

A Lesson About the Great Deptression. www.techteachers.com/depression.htm.

A People at War. http://www.archives.gov/exhibits/a_people_at_war/a_people_at _war.html

The Rise and Fall of Jim Crow. PBS. http://www.pbs.org/wnet/jimcrow/.

Dealing with History, Political Correctness, and Other Sensitive Issues

I n her 1998 article in *Language Arts*, Julie E. Wollman-Bonilla (1998) tells about teaching a social studies lesson to a group of sixth graders as part of her application for a teaching position. At one point in the lesson, she read aloud from *Roll of Thunder, Hear My Cry*. She writes:

> Afterward, the principal told me he was impressed with my courage in reading aloud from Taylor's powerful and honest book. This surprised me; I hadn't considered my choice courageous. I was simply trying to help the predominantly white sixth-graders recognize and think critically about racism. (287)

Nearly a decade later, she read aloud from the novel to a group of graduate students. One student responded, "Of course, you'd never read this book in a classroom of children" (287).

Wollman-Bonilla reports that such reactions are not at all unusual. In her more recent work with in-service teachers, she's received many negative comments about *Roll of Thunder*'s place in the curriculum. One teacher said, "I don't like books that describe racism and discrimination. It's a negative message. I don't want children to know that this could happen. It's so cruel" (290). Here are other comments from teachers Wollman-Bonilla has worked with:

- "I would never use a book in my classroom that talked about race like this. We're all the same. We shouldn't be pointing out racial differences" (291).

- "Reading it would make children think I feel like the white people in the book. I don't want them to think I use the word 'nigger'" (291).

- "I would never use this book if I had black students in my class. We should treat everyone the same" (291).

- "If I had to use this book I would change some of the words to make it less racist" (291).

Most teachers who have used *Roll of Thunder, Hear My Cry* or any of Mildred D. Taylor's books are surprised, perhaps even shocked, when they hear that many of Taylor's books have been attacked by parents or church groups demanding that the books be banned from schools. According to the American Library Association (ALA), *Roll of Thunder, The Friendship,* and *Mississippi Bridge* have been formally challenged several times since 1993, and *Roll of Thunder* ranked ninth on the ALA's list of the ten most challenged books of 2002 for the novel's "insensitivity, racism, and offensive language." According to the ALA's Office for Intellectual Freedom, "nationwide, [*Roll of Thunder*] faces at least a few challenges every year, mostly from black parents who don't like the language" ("Success Stories" 2004).

Here is a sampling of the challenges to Taylor's books:

- In 2004, the Seminole County School Board (Oviedo, Florida) decided to keep *Roll of Thunder* as part of middle school curriculum. It had been challenged by the parents of a thirteen-year-old seventh grader because they "thought the novel was as controversial as sex education materials and should be handled the same way—given to students only after parents had signed permission slips" ("Success Stories" 2004).

- In 2004, a parent of a middle school student in Cartersville, Georgia, challenged the use of *Roll of Thunder* in the middle school curriculum. (personal e-mail correspondence)

- In 2004, a black family in Guilderland, New York, wanted *Roll of Thunder* removed from the district curriculum because of fears that the novel would incite racial tension. (personal e-mail correspondence)

- In 2002, a black parent challenged the use of *Mississippi Bridge* in a fifth-grade class in North Carolina, claiming that the book's use of the N-word made it racially motivated and inappropriate for school use (Suhor 2002, 7).

- In 2002, a black parent in Illinois requested that *Roll of Thunder* be banned from use in grades 9–11 because of its racial content (Suhor 2002, 7).

- In 2001, after complaints from a parent that "the language is rough for a fourth grader" and "there's nothing positive in it. It's riddled with prejudice," a Henrico County (Sandston, Virginia) review committee voted to retain *Mississippi Bridge* in the school library (*Newsletter on Intellectual Freedom* 2001, 174).

- In 2000, in Huntsville, Alabama, "James Dawson, former Alabama A&M dean, current casket salesman and member of the Huntsville Board of Education . . . decreed that Mildred D. Taylor's award-winning 1973 novel, *Roll of Thunder, Hear My Cry*, isn't suitable for Chapman Elementary School's library because it uses racial slurs in dialogue to make points about racism" (*Newsletter on Intellectual Freedom* 2000, 47).

- In 1998, parents demanded that the Oakley (California) Union School District remove *Roll of Thunder* from O'Hara Park Middle School classrooms. "The controversy began when eleven-year-old Quinn Ellis came home crying after school in early April. His sixth-grade teacher read a passage from *Roll of Thunder* and 'read that "N" word out loud; and when she did, everyone turned around and looked at me,' said Quinn, who is black. 'I felt very uncomfortable. I felt it was a racial slur'" (*Newsletter on Intellectual Freedom* 1998, 107).

- In 1997, "Prince George's [Maryland] County Board of Education rejected a proposal for a committee to review reading lists for students and remove books considered offensive." A supporter of the measure said censorship is sometimes appropriate. The issue was brought to her attention by parents who objected to Theodore Taylor's *The Cay*, and she read examples from *The Cay*, which she claimed had 'no redeeming value,' and from Mildred D. Taylor's *The Friendship* to support the proposal" (*Newsletter on Intellectual Freedom* 1997, 149).

- In 1993, *Roll of Thunder* was removed from the ninth-grade reading list at Arcadia (Louisiana) High School after a group of parents wrote a letter to a local newspaper complaining that the novel was antiwhite. One parent said "black students openly taunted white students when the passages were read in class" (*Newsletter on Intellectual Freedom* 1993, 72).

Most of the complaints about Taylor's books can be traced to the current trend to attempt to govern language and behavior in modern society. Though the original intention of politically correct speech was noble, and even necessary, the overzealous or thoughtless application of PC has created problems for teachers, librarians, and books. Editor and critic Hazel Rochman (1993) has complained about the negative results of PC on libraries: "There are PC watchdogs eager to strip from the library shelves anything that presents a group as less than perfect. The ethnic character must always be strong, dignified, courageous, loving, sensitive, and wise" (17). Of course, plenty of books exist that perpetuate racial stereotypes or that reveal their racist bias through their representation of people of color, and the "PC watchdogs" have helped to identify the problems with those books. Unfortunately, however, many worthwhile books, including most of Mildred D. Taylor's, have been caught up in the PC sweep. Responsible authors and publishers want to produce books that benefit young readers, including books about all kinds of Americans, but, as Rochman points out, it's not as simple as it may seem:

> The paradox is that if we give young people didactic tracts, or stories so bland that they offend nobody, we're going to make them read even less. For books to give pleasure, there has to be tension and personality, laughter and passionate conflict. That's what will grab kids and touch them deeply—and make them want to read. (20)

The great majority of reasonable parents aren't looking for more bland, didactic books, but in their zeal to protect their children, they sometimes attack books that, ironically, would benefit these children by educating them about race and racial issues.

The examples above are ample evidence of the kinds of objections being leveled against Taylor's books these days, and teachers who plan to use them as required reading should be aware of the potential problems doing so may raise. A handful of parents object to Taylor's representation of Mississippi history. Others feel that the painful and sometimes cruel scenes in Taylor's books are too powerful for young readers. Some white parents don't like how white characters are represented; some black parents dislike Taylor's representation of black characters. And other parents, black and white, object to Taylor's use of the incendiary racist label *nigger*. Any combination of these concerns can lead to a challenge, and teachers must be prepared to meet those challenges.

Taylor's use of the N-word is the root of most challenges to her books, and it's an objection that must be carefully considered and thoughtfully responded to. The N-word is a powerful, contemporary racial epithet, and teachers who downplay or ignore its power risk offending some students and perhaps being forbidden to use her books. Marylee Hengstebeck's 1993 essay on racism in *The Adventures of Huckleberry Finn* presents an argument that English teachers must recognize. After considering the common defenses for using Twain's novel in her classes despite its potential to create discomfort for her black students, she comes to the conclusion that she can no longer use the novel:

> When one is confronted with the feelings of black students who can speak for themselves, all arguments, academic and otherwise, quickly grind to a halt. How am I supposed to explain to black students that they will be embarrassed/humiliated so that I can educate their fellow white students about racism? The whole idea seems racist at the core. (32)

Mark Franek and Nyaka NiiLampti (2005) present a scenario that replicates the feelings black students may experience when having to read *Huckleberry Finn* in English class. It's a situation teachers ought to consider carefully when selecting any novel that uses the N-word:

> The N-word keeps piling up. You've stopped reading, however, relying instead on the relative anonymity of class discussions and instincts you've honed from countless experiences as a black kid navigating through a predominantly white

environment. Your school has tricked you: Either you read the novel word for word, suffering a profoundly distasteful complicity in the process, or you fail. (21)

These two articles will help teachers understand the root of the majority of the objections to Taylor's books; there is no discounting the inflammatory force of the N-word.

The presence of that inflammatory word, however, probably doesn't justify dismissing Taylor's books from a school or class curriculum. The word is a concern, but it's a concern that can be responded to. When dealing with questions or challenges about the place of Taylor's books in the school library or curriculum, it may be helpful to know that the author herself is well aware of the objections that have been raised about her books. Here are some of her comments about the issue:

> In recent years, because of my concern about our "politically correct" society, I have found myself hesitating when using words that would have been spoken during the period in which my books are set. But just as I have had to be honest with myself in the telling of all my stories, I realized that I also must be true to the feelings of the people about whom I write, and I must be true to the stories told. My father and the other storytellers told my family's history truly, and it is their history that I have related in my books. When there was humor, my family passed it on. When there was tragedy, they pass it on. When the words hurt, they passed them on. My stories will not be "politically correct," so there are those who will be offended by them, but, as we all know, racism is offensive.
>
> It is not polite, and it is full of pain.
>
> I remember the pain. (2004, 8)

In her reader's note to *The Land*, Taylor writes:

> Although there are those who wish to ban my books because I have used language that is painful, I have chosen to use the language that was spoken during the period, for I refuse to whitewash history. The language was painful and life was painful for many African Americans, including my family. (2001a, xi)

She also responds to parents' concerns in her foreword to the twenty-fifth anniversary edition of *Roll of Thunder, Hear My Cry*:

> When I have heard such sentiments, I have been greatly disturbed. I have also been greatly disturbed at the possibility that any child has been hurt by my words.

> As a parent, I understand not wanting a child to hear painful words. But also as a parent I do not understand trying to prevent a child from learning about a history that is part of America, a history about a family representing millions of families who are strong and loving and who remain united and strong, despite the obstacles they face. (2001b, xii)

Parents or others who challenge the use of Taylor's books in schools might benefit from knowing that Taylor is African American and that she holds herself to the highest ideals of writing. The racist characters, cruel events, and painful language in her books are not intended to be inflammatory or hurtful; rather, these elements create a sense of reality, a careful depiction of the lives Taylor and her family led in the days before the civil rights movement. Taylor hopes that young readers will identify with the nobility of the Logans and be repulsed by the cruelty of the Logans' antagonists. In the reader's note to *The Land*, she explains her intent:

> Since writing my first book, *Song of the Trees*, it has been my wish to have readers walk in the shoes of the Logan family, who are based on my family, and to feel what they felt. It has been my wish that by understanding this family and what they endured, there would be further understanding of what millions of families endured, and there would also be a further understanding of why there was a Civil Rights Movement, a movement that changed our nation. (2001c, xi)

Taylor also hopes that her stories will educate today's young readers about the real history of blacks in the United States, a history that today's students may find unbelievable. In the foreword to the twenty-fifth anniversary edition of *Roll of Thunder, Hear My Cry* she writes:

> Today, however, younger generations have no experience of that time when signs over restroom doors, signs over water fountains, in restaurant windows and hotels said: WHITE ONLY, COLORED NOT ALLOWED. Today's generation of children, as well as many of their parents and teachers, have not had to endure such indignities or even worse aspects of racism that once pervaded America, and I am grateful for that. But, unfortunately, as we all know, racism still exists. (2001b, xi)

The widespread use of her books in schools around the country suggests that teachers and librarians do recognize the positive potential of the Logan family stories and that they see that these stories may help overcome the racism that still exists in America.

Mildred D. Taylor's personal experience has taught her the effects of racism, yes, but it has also taught her the power that parents and healthy families can wield to overcome the harmful effects of hate and racism. Her stories don't endorse racism or glorify racists, but they do represent a part of American history that should not be minimized or forgotten. Taylor rarely grants interviews, but in 2001—in her first interview in more than a decade—she felt compelled to defend her novels against the recent PC attacks on her use of language and her depiction of blacks in the 1930s:

> As a parent, I do understand people trying to protect their children from pain. What I do not understand is denying their children their heritage. I am concerned that people don't want their children to hear the truth. When *Roll of Thunder* first came out twenty-five years ago, there were white families who criticized it, saying, "Oh, this would never have happened." And, of course, it had happened. Now the same thing is going on with black families who don't want their children to hear the "n" word and to hear about the truth. How can I tell a story about this period in our history without using this word? Without talking about the racist views and the way people were treated back then? Some black parents don't even want their children to know that black people were second-class citizens in the past and that they had to react in a certain way just to survive. (Rochman 2001, 221)

The stories of the Logan family may be one of the most effective ways for young readers to understand what life was like for blacks in America before 1954, to feel the pain and the awful weight of racial oppression. This awareness, though unpleasant, shameful, and even painful, may be instrumental in helping students mature into adults who will stand for equality and against discrimination.

Teachers or librarians might want to point out that the issue of protecting children from harsh realities also comes up in Taylor's fiction. In *Roll of Thunder*, Mama is criticized by Miss Crocker, Cassie's teacher, for giving in to Cassie and Little Man's objections to the hand-me-down textbooks from the white schools. Rather than object to or subvert the racist condescension, Miss Crocker thinks black children must learn to accept racism and discrimination. She tells Mama, "Well, I just think you're spoiling those children, Mary. They've got to learn how things are sometime." Mama, perhaps reflecting Taylor's own attitude, replies,

"Maybe so, but that doesn't mean they have to accept them . . . and maybe we don't either" (30). Later in the novel, the Logans are listening to Mr. Morrison tell the story of how night men murdered his parents. The Logan children flinch in fear as the story unfolds, and Mama tries to stop the tale before it upsets them. Cassie's father recognizes Mama's desire to shield her children from the awful details, "but Papa enfolded her slender hand in his and said quietly, 'These are things they need to hear, baby. It's their history'" (148). A similar scene appears in *Let the Circle Be Unbroken* when Cassie wants to accompany Miz Lee Annie Lees in her attempt to register to vote. The situation in town is tense and dangerous, and Cassie's parents realize that Miz Lee Annie Lees' application might trigger racist violence. In responding to Big Ma and Uncle Hammer's objections to Cassie's request to go to Strawberry, Mama says, "This thing she's wanting to do, it could be something she *needs* to see" (333). Mama goes on to point out:

> "I'm just as scared as anybody about walking up to that registrar's office talking about voting. But I've got this feeling. Cassie's seen so much . . . learned so much about what it means to be black in these past few years. She's nearly witnessed a lynching. She's seen a boy sentenced to death. . . . This thing Mrs. Lee Annie wants to do, it's foolish perhaps, but it's something to be proud of too. If Cassie witnessed it, it could just mean a lot to her one day." (333)

Like Papa in *Roll of Thunder*, Mama realizes that racist experiences will be painful but essential in her daughter's education and maturity. Seeing the ugly reality of racial hatred and discrimination is the only way Cassie can be prepared to live— and survive—in a racist society.

As Cassie has gotten older, of course, she's had her fill of racist experience, and in *The Road to Memphis*, she acknowledges the pain, not the educational value, of being an oppressed minority in Mississippi. While the Aames brothers are tormenting Clarence, she reports, "A little ridicule wasn't supposed to hurt. But it did. It sliced like a knife" (118). Teachers should not forget that reading about racism can be painful.

Teachers dealing with challenges to Taylor's books should take heart that praise for the Logan stories greatly outweighs complaints. In describing the significance of Taylor's work on the occasion of her winning the inaugural NSK Neustadt Prize of Children's literature in 2003, Robert Con Davis-Undiano (2004) wrote:

Taylor stood up amid a sea of white students to tell the counternarrative of black heroism and perseverance that she knew to be the truth. Finally, it is in her novels that she supplies the missing, nuanced view of African American society as she knows it, displaying black culture's range of complexity and sophistication. (13)

Rather than harming black children or reinforcing stereotypes of blacks among white children, Taylor's stories present an honest, uplifting image of black culture. It's an image that, sadly, is underrepresented in literature. It's also an image that can have a powerful positive effect on black readers. KaaVonia Hinton's first encounter with one of Taylor's books had a dramatic effect on her:

When my eighth-grade teacher, new to the profession and to our district, shared Mildred Taylor's *Roll of Thunder, Hear My Cry* with the class . . . it was a pivotal time for me. For the first time in my life, I realized I was not alone in the world. There were other black girls having experiences similar to mine, and some had grown up and written them down. . . . This one simple act—handing me a book written by and about blacks—changed my life. (Hinton and Berry 2004/2005, 285)

Because they show black characters acting nobly and courageously, Taylor's books often have a profound influence on readers, especially black readers whose reading has been limited to books by white authors.

Of course, Taylor's stories have had a profound effect on other readers as well. Kathy Neustadt Hankin (2005) gives one white reader's impression of the merit of Taylor's books:

Mildred Taylor writes about good and bad, strong and evil, right and wrong, and, what is ultimately the saddest part of all, she writes the truth about our civil rights history. Her books deserve a place in every library, classroom, and history class and should be used to explain the way it was, the way it shouldn't have been, and how we can work together to make sure it never is that way again. (5)

Hankin's praise of Taylor's stories is not at all unusual and suggests why her books are so widely used in American schools.

Despite their popularity, however, it is likely that Taylor's books may provoke challenges from parents or local organizations, and it's important that teachers are prepared to deal with those challenges in objective, educationally sound ways. Fortunately, plenty of resources exist to help teachers defend their use of the

Logan stories. The National Council of Teachers of English (NCTE) has published rationales for *Roll of Thunder, Hear My Cry, The Road to Memphis*, and *The Land*. It also provides guidelines for writing rationales for books that will be used in schools. In addition to NCTE's support, the list of additional resources at the end of this chapter contains many articles and websites that can help teachers prepare thoughtful rationales for books and defend books against a variety of challenges. The wise teacher will become familiar with these resources.

Finally, here are ten suggestions that may help teachers and librarians deal with challenges to Taylor's—or any—books:

1. Before adopting a book, have a well-prepared rationale in place. A rationale explains the educational value of a book and justifies its use in a particular curriculum or program.

2. When a challenge comes, avoid being defensive. Earnestly seek to understand the challenger's concerns before you respond. In many cases, parents just want to know that their children's teacher has listened to and understood their concerns.

3. Be proactive. If you know a book is likely to provoke a negative reaction from some students or their parents, inform your students in advance of the issues or content in a book and explain the reasons the book is included in your curriculum. You might even consider sending home a permission-to-read form for parents to sign.

4. Instead of viewing censors as problems, view them as people who care about children and education.

5. Recognize the rights and responsibilities of parents. They, not you, are entitled to the final say of what their children will or won't read.

6. Confrontations over books can become emotional, and those emotions tend to block communication. Control your emotions and be willing to talk, civilly and maturely, about the issues.

7. Attacks on books frequently degenerate into attacks on teachers, and the assault can feel quite personal. Avoid taking the matter personally. Remember, the challengers' main concerns are the same as yours: the welfare of their children/your students.

8. Be willing to compromise. With all the wonderful books in the world, there is no single text that every student simply must read; as wonderful as Taylor's books are, they may not be suitable for all students. For every required book, prepare in advance a list of acceptable alternate readings.

9. Follow the guidelines for the adoption and removal of books recommended by professional organizations like NCTE, the American Library Association (ALA), and the International Reading Association (IRA).

10. Finally, throughout the process—from writing the rationale to defending the book—be thoroughly professional. Follow school, district, state, and professional guidelines for book selection and use (and when in doubt consult with) professional organizations like ALA, NCTE, and the National Coalition Against Censorship.

Mildred D. Taylor's books are wonderfully written, powerful stories that have much to offer students of all ages and all races. In today's PC culture, it's likely that challenges to her books will occur, but with a little foresight and preparation, teachers and librarians can ensure the continued presence of her books in classrooms and libraries.

Works Cited and Additional Resources

Print Sources

Brooks, Wanda, and Gregory Hampton. 2005. "Safe Discussions Rather Than Firsthand Encounters: Adolescents Examine Racism Through One Historical Text." *Children's Literature in Education* 36 (1) (March): 83–98.

Davis-Undiano, Robert Con. 2004. "Mildred D. Taylor and the Art of Making a Difference." *World Literature Today*, May–August: 11–13.

Dilg, Mary A. 1995. "The Opening of the American Mind: Challenges in the Cross-Cultural Teaching of Literature." *English Journal* 84 (3) (March): 18–25.

Franek, Mark, and Nyaka NiiLampti. 2005. "Shoot the Author, Not the Reader." *English Journal* 94 (6) (July): 20–22.

Hankin, Kathy Neustadt. 2005. "The Vast Potential of Human Possibilities." *World Literature Today*, January–April: 5.

"Harry Potter Is Most Challenged Fourth Year in a Row." 2003. *Newsletter on Intellectual Freedom* 52 (2) (March) [also at https://members.ala.org/nif/v52n2/harrypotter.html].

Henderson, Laretta. 2005. "The Black Arts Movement and African American Young Adult Literature: An Evaluation of Narrative Style." *Children's Literature in Education* 36 (4) (December): 299–323.

Hengstebeck, Marylee. 1993. "*Huck Finn*, Slavery, and Me." *English Journal* 82 (7) (November): 32.

Hinton, KaaVonia, and Theodora Berry. 2004/2005. "Literacy, Literature, and Diversity." *Journal of Adolescent and Adult Literacy* 48 (4) (December/January): 284–88.

Jasper, Gigi. 1998. "Multiculturally Challenged." *English Journal* 88 (2) (November): 93–97.

Lowe, Barbara. 2004. "Race Relations in Newbery Award Novels, 1922–2000." Ph.D. diss., University of Mississippi.

Muhammad, Rashidah Jaami. 1996. "Value and Authenticity: Young Adult Readers Respond to African American Literature." Ph.D. diss., Michigan State University.

Newsletter on Intellectual Freedom. 1993. Vol. 42 (May).

Newsletter on Intellectual Freedom. 1997. Vol. 46 (September).

Newsletter on Intellectual Freedom. 1998. Vol. 47 (July).

Newsletter on Intellectual Freedom. 2000. Vol. 49 (March).

Newsletter on Intellectual Freedom. 2001. Vol. 50 (July).

Postal, Leslie. "Take Book Out of Schools in Seminole, Parents Ask." *Orlando Sentinel*, January 26, 2004 [also at www.ncac.org/education/20040126~FL Seminole_County~Roll_of_Thunder_Challenged_in_Seminole_County.cfm].

Rationales for Teaching Challenged Books. 1998. CD. Urbana, IL: National Council of Teachers of English.

Rees, David. 1980. "The Color of Skin: Mildred Taylor." In *The Marble in the Water,* 104–33. Boston: Horn Book.

Rochman, Hazel. 1993. *Against Borders: Promoting Books for a Multicultural World.* Chicago: American Library Association.

———. 2001. "The *Booklist* Interview: Mildred Taylor." *Booklist* 98 (2) (September 15): 221.

Smith, Karen Patricia. 1994. "A Chronicle of Family Honor: Balancing Rage and Triumph in the Novels of Mildred D. Taylor." In *African American Voices in*

Young Adult Literature: Tradition, Transition, Transformation, 247–76. Metuchen, NJ: Scarecrow.

Stallworth, B. Joyce, Louel Gibbons, and Leigh Fauber. 2006. "It's Not on the List: An Exploration of Teachers' Perspectives on Using Multicultural Literature." *Journal of Adolescent and Adult Literacy* 46 (6) (March): 478–89.

"Success Stories: Schools." 2004. *Newsletter on Intellectual Freedom* 53 (2) (March): 75–76.

Suhor, Charles. 2002. "Few Calls, More Book Bannings—Why?" *SLATE* 27 (3) (April): 1, 6–7.

Taylor, Mildred D. 1998. "Acceptance Speech for the 1997 ALAN Award." *The ALAN Review* 25 (Spring): 2–3 [also at http://scholar.lib.vt.edu/ejournals /ALAN/spring98/taylor.html].

———. 2001a. "Author's Note." In *The Land*, 371–75. New York: Dial.

———. 2001b. "Foreword." In *Roll of Thunder, Hear My Cry*, 25th Anniversary Ed., vii–xiv. New York: Phyllis Fogelman.

———. 2001c. "A Note to the Reader." In *The Land*, xii. New York: Dial.

———. "My Life as a Writer." 2004. *World Literature Today*, May–August: 7–10 [also at http://www.ou.edu/worldlit/onlinemagazine/SA2004/11608-03-May-Aug%20Taylor.pdf].

Taxel, Joel. 1997. "Multicultural Literature and the Politics of Reason." *Teachers College Record* 98 (3) (Spring): 417–48.

Wollman-Bonilla, Jule E. 1998. "Outrageous Viewpoints: Teachers' Criteria for Rejecting Works of Children's Literature." *Language Arts* 75 (4) (April): 287–95.

Zeeman, Kenneth L. 1997. "Grappling with Grendel: What We Did When the Censors Came." *English Journal* 86 (2) (February): 46–49.

Internet Sites

American Library Association Banned Books Week. www.ala.org/ala/oif /bannedbooksweek/bannedbooksweek.htm.

American Library Association Office for Intellectual Freedom. www.ala.org/oif.

"Censorship in the Classroom: Understanding Controversial Issues." IRA. www .reading.org/resources/tools/lessons/203.html.

"Letter from NCAC to Protest the Challenging of *Roll of Thunder, Hear My Cry*." January 26, 2004. www.ncac.org/education/related/20040126~FLSeminole_County~NCAC_Letter_to_Seminole_County_School_Board.cfm

National Coalition Against Censorship. www.ncac.org.
National Council of Teachers of English Anti-censorship Center. www.ncte.org /about/issues/censorship.

Literature Circle Resources

Beeghly, Dena G. 2005. "It's About Time: Using Electronic Literature Discussion Groups with Adult Learners." *Journal of Adolescent and Adult Literacy* 49 (1) (September): 12–21.

Callan, Rebecca. 2003. *Literature Circle Guide: Roll of Thunder, Hear My Cry.* Scholastic Teaching Resources.

Crowe, Chris. 2003. "Reading African American History and the Civil Rights Movement." *English Journal* 92 (3) (January): 131–34.

Dalie, Sandra Okura. 2001. "Students Becoming Real Readers: Literature Circles in High School English Classes." In *Teaching Reading in High School English Classes*, edited by Bonnie O. Ericson, 84–100. Urbana, IL: NCTE.

Daniels, Harvey. 2002. *Literature Circles: Voice and Choice in Book Clubs and Reading Groups*. Portland, ME: Stenhouse.

Daniels, Harvey, and Nancy Steineke. 2004. *Mini-Lessons for Literature Circles*. Portsmouth, NH: Heinemann.

Day, Jeni Pollack, et al. 2002. *Moving Forward with Literature Circles: How to Plan, Manage and Evaluate Literature Circles to Deepen Understanding and Foster a Love of Reading.* New York: Scholastic Professional Books.

Faust, Mark A., and Nancy Glenzer. 2000. "'I Could Read Those Parts Over and Over': Eighth Graders Rereading to Enhance Enjoyment and Learning with Literature." *Journal of Adolescent and Adult Literacy* 44 (3) (November): 234–39.

Hill, Bonnie Campbell, Nancy Johnson, and Katherine L. Schlick-Noe. 2000.

Literature Circles Resource Guide: Teaching Suggestions, Forms, Sample Book Lists, and Database. Norwood, MA: Christopher-Gordon.

Hill, Bonnie Campbell, Katherine L. Schlick Noe, and Janine A. King. 2003. *Literature Circles in Middle School: One Teacher's Journey.* Norwood, MA: Christopher-Gordon.

Lopez, Janet. "Literature Circles," LitSite Alaska. http://litsite.alaska.edu/uaa /workbooks/circlereading.html.

LiteratureCircles.com. www.litcircles.org.

Literature Circles Resource Center. fac-staff.seattleu.edu/kschlnoe/web /LitCircles/index.html.

McCann, Thomas M. 2003. "Imagine This: Using Scenarios to Promote Authentic Discussion." *English Journal* 92 (6) (July): 31–39.

Martin, Michelle H. 1998. "Exploring the Novels of Mildred Taylor: An Approach to Teaching the Logan Family Novels." *Teaching and Learning Literature* 7 (3) (January–February): 5–13.

Miller, Howard M. 1997. "Beyond 'Multicultural Moments.'" *English Journal* 86 (5) (September): 88–90.

Moen, Christine Boardman. 2004. *25 Reproducible Literature Circle Role Sheets.* Carthage, IL: Teaching and Learning.

O'Connor, Beth. "Traveling the Road to Freedom Through Research and Historical Fiction." ReadWriteThink. www.readwritethink.org/lessons /lesson_view.asp?id=864.

Shea, Mary E. "Heroes Around Us." ReadWriteThink. www.readwritethink.org /lessons/lesson_view.asp?id=171.

Stix, Andi. "Mixing It Up: A Multilevel Book Room and Flexible Literature Circles." www.interactiveclassroom.com/articles.htm.

"Suggestions for Literature Circles in the Middle Grades." The MiddleWeb Listserv. www.middleweb.com/MWLresources/litcircles.html.

Wehrmann, Kari Sue. 2000. "How to Differentiate Instruction: Baby Steps—A Beginner's Guide." *Educational Leadership* 58 (1) (September): 20–23 [also found at www.nea.org/teachexperience/diffk021218.html].

Wilhelm, Jeffrey D., Tanya Baker, and Julie Dube. 2001. *Strategic Reading: Guiding Students to Lifelong Literacy, K–12.* Portsmouth, NH: Heinemann.

Resources on Mildred D. Taylor

Print Sources

Crowe, Chris. 1999. *Presenting Mildred D. Taylor.* New York: Twayne.

Davis-Undiano, Robert Con. 2004. "Mildred D. Taylor and the Art of Making a Difference." *World Literature Today*, May–August, 11–13.

Harper, Mary Turner. 1988. "Merger and Metamorphosis in the Fiction of Mildred D. Taylor." *Children's Literature Association Quarterly* 13 (1): 75–80.

Houghton, Gillian. 2005. *Mildred Taylor.* New York: Rosen.

Johnson, Nancy J., and Cyndi Giorgis. 2006. "Talking with Mildred D. Taylor." *Book Links* 15 (6) (July): 44–45.

Kirk, Susanne Porter. 1997. "Mildred Delois Taylor." In *Writers for Young Adults*, vol. 3, edited by Ted Hipple, 273–82. New York: Scribner's.

Rees, David. 1980. "The Color of Skin: Mildred Taylor." In *The Marble in the Water*, 104–33. Boston: Horn Book.

Rochman, Hazel. 2001. "The *Booklist* Interview: Mildred Taylor." *Booklist* (September 15): 221.

Scales, Pat. 2003. "Profile. Mildred D. Taylor: Keeper of Stories." *Language Arts* 80 (3) (January): 240–44.

Smith, Karen Patricia. 1994. "A Chronicle of Family Honor: Balancing Rage and Triumph in the Novels of Mildred D. Taylor." In *African American Voices in Young Adult Literature: Tradition, Transition, Transformation*, 247–76. Metuchen, NJ: Scarecrow.

Taylor, Mildred D. 1977. "Newbery Medal Acceptance Speech." *Horn Book Magazine* 53 (4) (August): 401–9.

———. 1988. "Mildred D. Taylor." In *Something About the Author Autobiography Series*, vol. 5, edited by Adele Sarkissian, 267–86. Detroit: Gale Research.

———. 1989. "Acceptance Speech for the *Boston Globe–Horn Book* Award for *The Friendship*." *Horn Book Magazine* 65 (2) (March/April): 179–82.

———. 1990. "Growing Up with Stories." *Booklist,* December 1, 740–41.

———. 1998. "Acceptance Speech for the 1997 ALAN Award." *The ALAN Review* 25 (Spring): 2–3 [also at http://scholar.lib.vt.edu/ejournals/ALAN /spring98/taylor.html].

———. 2004. "My Life as a Writer." *World Literature Today*, May–August, 7–10 [also at www.ou.edu/worldlit/onlinemagazine/SA2004/11608-03-May-Aug%20Taylor.pdf].

Video Sources

Meet the Newbery Author: Mildred D. Taylor. 1991. Videocassette. Miller-Brody, producer [American School Publications #004614].

Mildred D. Taylor: Roll of Thunder, Hear My Cry. 1991. Videocassette. Original release 1988. Films for the Humanities and Sciences [#2800].

Internet Sites

"Examining the African American Family Through the Eyes of Women Authors." Yale-New Haven Teachers Institute. www.yale.edu/ynhti /curriculum/units/1999/1/99.01.10.x.html.

Internet Sites, Discussion Groups, and ERIC Citations on Mildred D. Taylor. www.indiana.edu/~reading/ieo/bibs/taylor.html.

Mildred D. Taylor Message Board. www.allreaders.com/Board.asp?BoardID =26620.

Mildred Taylor Teacher Resource File. http://falcon.jmu.edu/~ramseyil /taylor.htm.

"Mildred Taylor." The Mississippi Writers Page. www.olemiss.edu/mwp/dir /taylor_mildred/

"Mildred Taylor." www.indiana.edu/~reading/ieo/bibs/taylor.html [also at www.indiana.edu/%7Ereading/ieo/bibs/taylor.html].

"A Teacher's Guide to *The Land* and Other Books by Mildred D. Taylor." www.teachervision.fen.com/page/31177.html.

Mildred Taylor. Lesson Plans for *Roll of Thunder, Hear My Cry*. www .webenglishteacher.com/mtaylor.html.

Mildred D. Taylor. The Mississippi Writers and Musicians Project at Starkville
    High School. http://shs.starkville.k12.ms.us/mswm
    /MSWritersAndMusicians/writers/MildredDTaylor/Taylor.html.

Prereading Activities for Mildred D. Taylor's Stories

Opinionnaire

In the space at the left, write "A" if you agree, "D" if you disagree.

_____ 1. In order to be financially secure, it's important for people to own their own houses and land.

_____ 2. All people in America are protected fairly and equally by American laws.

_____ 3. People suffering from poverty also suffer from lack of education.

_____ 4. Strong families can help children survive and learn from difficult or painful experiences.

_____ 5. In stories about the South, the villains are always white men.

_____ 6. In the period after the Civil War called Reconstruction, African Americans in southern states enjoyed all the rights and freedoms of American citizens.

_____ 7. It is a parent's responsibility to shield his or her children from the unpleasant realities of life.

_____ 8. During the Great Depression, all people were poor; therefore, all people faced the same problems.

_____ 9. People who are honest and who work hard will be successful regardless of who they are or where they live.

_____ 10. People from different backgrounds cannot become good friends.

What Would You Do?

Put yourself in the situation of an African American boy or girl living in Mississippi in the 1930s during a period of American history known as the Great Depression. You live with your family on a small farm and, unlike most of your neighbors, your family owns your land. Even though you own land, you're still extremely poor. Your white neighbors are jealous of your family, and the richest man in the area is constantly trying to steal your land. Most white people in the area have racist attitudes, and the cruelest people look for ways to scare or harm African Americans.

Review the list below, and place a check in the box of actions that you would take or that you would encourage your family to take.

☐ Sell the land and move to a safer community.

☐ Demand protection from the local sheriff.

☐ Carry a gun at all times.

☐ Avoid all contact with racists.

☐ Be very kind to all racists.

☐ Get the best education possible.

☐ Try to make friends with the people who are cruel.

☐ Work hard to please everyone.

☐ Stay home and read books all the time.

☐ Campaign for politicians who would make life better.

☐ With neighbors, form a group of people who will publicly protest against racism and inequality.

☐ Avoid shopping in stores owned by racists.

☐ Be willing to risk your life to protect your family members.

☐ Sell part of your land to the rich white man, hoping that he'll stop trying to steal all of it.

☐ Endure the abuse and racist treatment without complaint.

☐ Find sneaky ways to undermine the racist system and rules.

Just Imagine

The year is 1933, and the place is Mississippi. You live in a small log cabin on a poor farm with your parents, one grandmother, and three brothers. You're the second oldest child, and you're smart and very independent. As an African American family, you are respected by your African American neighbors but despised by most white people. You and your brothers attend a poor African American school, and you must walk there—several miles—each day. Your father works on the farm but also works on the railroad and is gone for much of the year. Your family is constantly on the brink of disaster. Money is scarce, and what little your father earns goes to pay the interest on the mortgage for your small farm. Nearly all of your food comes from your own garden. Many of the white people in the area are cruel racists, and sometimes at night you can't sleep because of the sounds of roving Night Riders who are out looking for African Americans to torment or kill. Jim Crow laws severely limit your freedoms and guarantee white people that they can get away with almost any crime against African Americans. Your family can barely pay the mortgage, and a local white man, an extremely wealthy landowner, is always trying to steal or buy your land. You and your family know that you must be very careful around white people; if any of you step out of line, you could be injured or even killed. Despite these difficult circumstances, you and your family love this place and are determined to do whatever you can to stay here.

What kinds of activities would be most likely to anger the local racists?

What kinds of things might racists do to make your life more difficult?

What might happen if you befriended a white kid your age?

How might your school be different from the white school?

What might happen to your teacher if she tries to make your school equal to the white school?

In what ways might you and your family subvert the racist laws and traditions?

How could you determine who is trustworthy and who isn't?

What might happen to you or your parents if you openly fought against the inequality in your community?

If you or your family became a target of the local racists, what could you do to protect yourself?

What would happen if your father disappears or is killed?

Then and Now, Me and Them

Consider how your life differs from the lives of African Americans your age who lived in the South during the Great Depression. Write a brief description for each category. Use your best guess to describe "Their Then."

	My Now	Their Then
school		
home		
parents' employment		
how police treat me		
freedom of expression		
freedom of travel		
hobbies		
entertainment		
clothing		

friends		
dreams of the future		
heroes		
fears		
talents		
favorite food		
books		
music		
treats and snacks		

Terms to Know and Show

Select ten or more of the terms below. Find an accurate definition of each, and write it down in your own words. After you have a definition, find a good example of each term that you've defined. Your good example might be anything that helps you or someone who is unfamiliar with the term understand what it means. Photographs, drawings, newspaper articles, or encyclopedia entries are examples of possible good examples of the terms you choose.

Jim Crow

the Great Depression

the Mississippi Delta

sharecropping

tenant farming

racial segregation

Reconstruction

Ku Klux Klan

cotton farming

miscegenation laws

voter literacy tests

lynch laws

White Citizens' Councils

the Natchez Trace

mortgages

the New Deal

Farm Security Administration

carpetbaggers

Civilian Conservation Corps

Southern Tenant Farmers Union

the Scottsboro Boys

Plessy v. Ferguson

the Dred Scott Case

slavery

boycott

W. E. B. Dubois

Booker T. Washington

Fannie Lou Hamer

Malcolm X

Emmett Till

cotton gin

Uncle Tom

Questions for
Mildred D. Taylor Literature Circles

First Third of the Book

1. What is the significance of the title? As you started reading, what did it mean to you?
2. What is the setting of the story? How does Mildred D. Taylor introduce you to the setting?
3. Who is (are) the protagonist(s)? Describe he/she/them.
4. In your early reading, what do you perceive as the conflict of the story?
5. Does the story have an antagonist? If so, describe the person(s).
6. Who is the narrator? Why did Taylor choose that person to tell the story instead of someone else?
7. You can't judge a book by its cover, but we do, initially at least. What was your first impression of your book? What kind of story were you (are you) expecting?
8. What might happen to the main character by the end of the book?
9. What other books have you read by Taylor? What books have you read that are similar to this one? Briefly compare and contrast them.
10. What is the opening sentence of the story? Explain how, in your opinion,

the author came up with it. Is it an effective way to begin this story? Why/why not?

Middle Third of the Book

1. What are the conflicts in the story? List each separately and explain it.
2. What type of conflicts are in the story (e.g., man vs. man, man vs. nature, etc.)? List them and explain why you have categorized them as you have.
3. Which characters have changed since the beginning of the story? How have they changed? Why have they changed?
4. Place the characters in two categories: flat characters and round characters.
5. Explain how Taylor has characterized the protagonist and one other character. Give examples from the book.
6. What are your feelings toward the protagonist? What has Taylor done to create those feelings?
7. What has been your favorite scene so far in the story? Describe the scene and explain why you liked it.
8. Which parts of the story seem realistic? Which parts seem unrealistic? Explain your answers.
9. What has the protagonist done to overcome the conflict? Explain his or her actions.
10. What motivates the protagonist to act the way she or he does? Explain your answer; include references to the story.

Last Third of the Book

1. What was the theme of the story?
2. What symbols were used in the story? (Look for recurring objects, colors, settings, etc.)
3. What was the climax of the story? Explain it.
4. On the first set of questions, you listed what you thought were the conflicts of the story. Now that you've finished the book, were you right? What do you see as the major conflict of the book at this point?
5. How is the main conflict of the story resolved?
6. List and explain examples of situational and dramatic irony from the story.
7. Assuming that by now you know something about Mildred D. Taylor's life, what evidences of the author's personality (or background, beliefs, life, etc.) can you find in the book?

8. Which characters appealed to you the most? Why?
9. In your opinion, what were the best parts of the book? What parts would you like to see changed or left out completely?
10. Write a *TV Guide*–style blurb about this book. Limit yourself to two sentences.

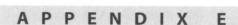

A P P E N D I X   E

★ What Do I Do After Literature Circle Reading and Discussion?

Suggested Intergroup and Whole-Class Activities

1. Create a master list of all the important characters in the Logan books. Include the name of the book(s) that the characters appear in.
2. Create a family tree/pedigree chart that contains all of the Logan characters.
3. Make a map of Mississippi in the 1880s. Place the towns mentioned in the books on the map.
4. Make a timeline that features key events from all of the Logan books. As an enhancement, include important events from American history as well.
5. Using Freytag's Pyramid as a template, diagram the plot of one of the stories in the Logan family saga. Compare your plot diagram with the plot diagrams of other Logan stories read by your classmates.
6. What is sharecropping? How did it work and what effect did it have on sharecroppers? Who are the sharecroppers in Taylor's books and what are their attitudes toward the system? How was a tenant farmer different from a sharecropper?
7. What is Jim Crow? What were the Black Codes? Find examples of these social policies in American history and in the Logan stories.
8. What was Reconstruction? How did it affect African Americans in the South? Who was opposed to it? Why were they opposed? What are some things those people did to undermine Reconstruction?
9. Look up information on the following real people: Frederick Douglass, Hiram Revels, Blanche Bruce, Ida B. Wells Barnett, Booker T. Washington,

W. E. B. DuBois, Lloyd Gaines, A. Philip Randolph, Emmett Till, Medgar Evers, James Chaney, Linda Brown, Thurgood Marshall, James Meredith, and Fannie Lou Hamer. Why are they important characters in Mississippi and/or African American history? Which of these people might be similar to characters in Taylor's stories?

10. The Fifteenth Amendment and the Civil Rights Act of 1875 were political attempts to provide equality for African Americans. How successful were these attempts? What other political efforts were tried from 1870 to 1940? Which ones had a direct effect on the Logan family or other characters in the Logan stories?

11. Learn about the 1892 U.S. Supreme Court ruling *Plessy v. Ferguson*. How did it reinforce the decision in the 1857 Dred Scott case? What effect did *Plessy v. Ferguson* have on African Americans in the South? Find examples of the results of that Supreme Court ruling that affect characters in the Logan stories.

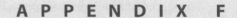

Responding to Mildred D. Taylor's Books

Alternative Responses

1. Based on the information you gain from reading Mildred D. Taylor's books, sketch a map of the area where the Logan family lives. You may not be able to accurately locate every place mentioned in the books, but you should have a general understanding of the geography around the Logan home. Some possible locations to include Great Faith Church and School, Jefferson Davis School, the Wallace store, the Rosa Lee, Soldiers Road and Bridge, surrounding plantations, Jackson, Strawberry.

2. In the acknowledgments to *The Land*, Taylor writes about a visit from her family: "As I cooked breakfast one morning, [my two uncles] and other family members gathered in the kitchen and soon, as always happens when my family gets together, the stories began. There were hilarious stories about my father, my uncles, and my aunts growing up on the family land in Mississippi. There were stories about my grandparents and great-uncles, and there were stories about my great-grandparents" (vii). Each of Taylor's books comes from stories like these. Ask your relatives if there are any stories from your family. Listen to these stories and choose one to learn well and retell. Retell the story to your siblings, parents, or cousins.

3. In the foreword to the twenty-fifth anniversary edition of *Roll of Thunder, Hear My Cry*, Taylor writes about the final book in the Logan family saga: "Now I have only one more story to tell about the Logan family. It is the story of the family in the North, the days of World War II, and the first seeds of the Civil Rights Movement" (xiii). Make a family tree of the Logans who

might be included in this novel. The novel is tentatively titled *Logan*; design a cover for that novel.

4. Select a scene from one of the Logan stories and write a newspaper account of the scene. For example, you could write an article that tells what happened when John Wallace shot Mr. Tom Bee in *The Friendship* or about the fire on the Logan farm that stopped the lynch mob in *Roll of Thunder, Hear My Cry*.

5. Using digital photos and images from various websites, like "African American Odyssey" (http://memory.loc.gov/ammem/aaohtml/aohome.html) and "America from the Great Depression to World War II: Photographs from the FSA-OWI, 1935–1945" (http://memory.loc.gov/ammem/fsowhome .html), create a collage that represents your favorite book by Mildred D. Taylor. Write a paragraph that explains how the photographs represent the story.

6. Create a PowerPoint presentation that summarizes one of the Logan family stories. Use text frames, photographs, and illustrations to complete the slide show.

7. With a partner, choose any two of Mildred D. Taylor's books and create two Venn diagrams. The first diagram should compare and contrast the characters in the two books. The second diagram should compare and contrast the plots of the two books.

8. Review the literary term *symbolism*. Then select one of Taylor's books and look through it for symbols. Make a list of the symbols; include where they appear in the story, what effect they have on the story, and what they might represent.

Creative Writing

1. All of Taylor's books are based on her extended family. Write your own short story based on your extended family. In order to do this, interview older relatives—grandmothers, grandfathers, older aunts and uncles—and ask them about their lives growing up. What stories do they remember? What stories do they remember their parents and grandparents telling about their childhoods? Choose one of these stories and write it as a short story.

2. Read some poetry for two voices (Paul Fleischman's *Joyful Noise: Poems for Two Voices* and *I Am Phoenix: Poems for Two Voices* are excellent examples) to understand the form and how poems like this are written and read. Then write some two-voice poems for characters from one of the Logan books.

Here are some suggested pairs: Stacey and Cassie, Big Ma and Paul-Edward, David and Mary, David and Hammer, Jeremy and Stacey, T. J. and Stacey, Clarence and Sissy, Moe and Cassie, Jeremy and his father, Mr. Jamison and David. In addition to writing poems for characters from the same story, consider other possibilities: two places (the Rosa Lee and the bridge, Strawberry and Jackson, Jackson and Memphis, the court house and the Barnett Mercantile, etc.), the same character from two different time periods (younger and older Stacey, T. J., Cassie, David, Caroline, etc.), or two objects important in the stories (Stacey's car and one of Hammer's cars, the bus and the bridge, etc.).

3. Choose one of Taylor's books and identify the narrator. Then choose another character in the book and retell a scene in the voice of the other character. For example, you could write about Solomon Bradley meeting Cassie (in *The Road to Memphis*) from Solomon's point of view, or you could write about the Barnett Mercantile robbery (in *Roll of Thunder, Hear My Cry*) from T. J. Avery's perspective.

4. Choose five characters from one of the Logan stories and write "name poems" for each of them. For an example of this kind of name poem, go to http://www.eastern.edu/publications/emme/1999spring/bloom.html.

5. Read an encyclopedia entry about Malcolm X, Helen Keller, Theodore Roosevelt, or some other well-known American. After becoming familiar with the encyclopedia style of writing, write an entry for Mildred D. Taylor or one of her characters.

6. In Taylor's books, sometimes one of the Logan children is forced to apologize to someone else. At other times, one of the villains in the book does something that he or she should apologize for. Choose a character and a situation from one of the stories, and imagine that you're that character. In the voice of that character, write a letter of apology to the person you hurt, offended, or angered.

Responding to Mildred D. Taylor

1. Read some of the statements Mildred D. Taylor has made about her books. For example, read the foreword to the twenty-fifth anniversary edition of *Roll of Thunder, Hear My Cry* or the reader's note in *The Land*. You might also read her acceptance speech for the 1997 ALAN Award (http://scholar.lib .vt.edu/ejournals/ALAN/spring98/taylor.html). After reading one or more of these statements, write a letter to Taylor sharing your own thoughts about

the issues she mentions. Your letter should be at least one page long and should show her that you have read at least one of her books and thought carefully about it. After you write the letter, mail it to her:

Ms. Mildred D. Taylor

c/o Dial Books for Young Readers

345 Hudson Street

New York, New York 10014-3434

2. Find someone who remembers segregation and talk to him/her about what it was like to live in a segregated society. Ask him/her to share feelings about growing up amid racism. Do you believe that racism still exists and is growing? What evidence do you have for your belief? What examples of racism exist today?

3. Did you find Taylor's books painful to read? What incidents/events were painful? Did you understand racism better after reading Taylor's books? What understanding did you come to? Which characters/events/situations helped you better understand racism? Did you better understand the effects of racism on the racists themselves? Which characters/events/situations helped you better understand the effects of racism on the people propagating it?

4. Do you think Taylor's books should be removed from reading lists because of the language? Why do you think it's important to include the N-word in Taylor's works? Is there any justifiable reason for parents not to want their children to learn about history? How would you respond in the face of these calls for censorship? Do you think it is important for children to hear painful words? What value is there in this? How have you personally been affected by reading these books? Do you wish you hadn't read the language? Or are you glad that you did? What have you learned about American history by reading Taylor's novels?

5. All of Mildred D. Taylor's stories take place prior to the civil rights movement, yet she suggests that one of the reasons she's writing is to help readers better understand why there was a civil rights movement. What was the civil rights movement and what did it accomplish? How do her books help you understand the need for a civil rights movement? How do they help you appreciate what the movement accomplished? What characters/events/situations in her novels signal the coming of a civil rights movement (consider Cassie's first conversation with Solomon Bradley in *The Road to Memphis*, for example)?

6. What did you learn from Taylor's books about the importance of land ownership? Can you see, after reading her books, why land ownership would be
   so important to her? Does your family own land? What does it mean to
   you? Ask your parents, grandparents, or great-grandparents about their
   struggles to purchase land. Have they had to sacrifice in order to purchase
   land? If so, why did they do it?

Responding to the Books

1. Choose one of the following characters from Taylor's books: Cassie Logan,
   David Logan, Jeremy Simms, Moe Turner, T. J. Avery, Big Ma, or Stacey Logan.
   Complete the following after reading more than one of Taylor's books:
   a. Draw a picture of the character.
   b. Create a timeline of important events in that character's life.
   c. Write a letter from that character to any other character in the books.
       The letter should accurately reflect the character's personality and what
       he/she might really say in a letter.
   d. Write a brief essay in which you examine the ways the character you
       have chosen has changed over time and what brought about those
       changes.

2. Of all the Logan family books, only one is narrated by a non-Logan family
   member. In *Mississippi Bridge*, Jeremy Simms, the Logans' enigmatic white
   friend, narrates. Compare and contrast this story with those narrated by
   Cassie Logan. Some questions to consider in your comparison/contrast:
   a. How does Jeremy's narration compare with Cassie's? Find specific simi-
       larities and differences. You may want to draw a Venn diagram to help
       you compare and contrast the narration.
   b. Why did Taylor choose to have Jeremy narrate this story?
   c. How would the story be different if Cassie were narrating? Would she
       be able to tell this same story?

3. Choose one of the following themes that are present throughout Taylor's
   books (or choose another theme that you noticed appears in all of Taylor's
   works): the impact of racism in the South, the importance of family, the
   value of ownership (particularly land and automobile ownership), the need
   for and value of education, the power of peer pressure, the role of friendship
   on individuals' lives, the role of a supportive community on the lives of its
   members. After choosing a theme:

a. List events from each of the novels your group read that correlate with the theme you've chosen. For example, if you chose the role of friendship, you might list the following events: Jeremy hiding Moe in his truck after Moe attacked the Aameses (*The Road to Memphis*); the Logan children risking their lives to help out T. J. Avery on the night of the murder and robbery at the Barnett Mercantile in Strawberry (*Roll of Thunder*); Mr. Jamison's willingness to represent T. J. in court (*Let the Circle Be Unbroken*); etc.

b. After compiling your list, discuss with your group the events and what Taylor is saying about that particular theme by including them. For example, your discussion about the role of friendship might include the following:

1. A recognition that friendship between the races (Jeremy with the Logans, Mr. Jamison with the Logans) can only go so far. According to Taylor, during the time in which the novels are set, there couldn't be a lasting, binding friendship between races.

2. The understanding that friendship sometimes isn't enough to save a life. T. J.'s actions have drastic consequences despite the friendship offered him by Stacey.

3. An understanding that friendships are sometimes betrayed. The Logans feel like Jeremy betrays their friendship when he participates in the hunt for Harris with his cousins.

c. Continue your discussion by talking about how one of Taylor's themes plays out in the lives of your group members. For example, you could talk about your own experiences with friends. Have you had any similar experiences to the ones presented in Taylor's novels? How have friendships affected the members of your group positively or negatively?

d. Finally, report on your discussion by having each group member write a paragraph responding to the discussion. Some questions to consider in the paragraph:

1. What did I learn?

2. What did Taylor present in her novels that I could connect to?

3. What did I find out about my group members that I didn't know before?

Related Reading

Fiction

Armstrong, William H. *Sounder*. New York: Harper & Row, 1969.

Brady, Laurel. *Say You Are My Sister*. New York: HarperCollins, 2000.

Chesnutt, Charles W. *The House Behind the Cedars*. New York: Penguin Classics, 1993.

Crowe, Chris. *Mississippi Trial, 1955*. New York: Dial, 2002.

Curtis, Christopher Paul. *Bud, Not Buddy*. New York: Random House, 1999.

Fuqua, Jonathan Scott. *Darby*. New York: Candlewick, 2002.

Hesse, Karen. *Out of the Dust*. New York: Scholastic, 1997.

———. *Witness*. New York: Scholastic, 2001.

Krisher, Trudy. *Spite Fences*. New York: Delacorte, 1994.

Lee, Harper. *To Kill a Mockingbird*. New York: Warner, 1960.

Meyer, Carolyn. *White Lilacs*. San Diego: Gulliver, 1993.

Moses, Sheila P. *The Legend of Buddy Bush*. New York: Margaret K. McElderry, 2003.

Myers, Anna. *Tulsa Burning*. New York: Walker, 2002.

Nolan, Han. *A Summer of Kings*. New York: Harcourt, 2006.

Peck, Richard. *The River Between Us*. New York: Dial, 2003.

Rabe, Berniece. *Hiding Mr. McMulty*. San Diego: Harcourt, 1997.

Ritter, John H. *Choosing Up Sides*. Philomel, 1998.

Ryan, Pam Muñoz. *Esperanza Rising*. New York: Scholastic, 2000.

Schmidt, Gary D. *Lizzie Bright and the Buckminster Boy*. New York: Clarion, 2004.

Sebestyen, Ouida. *Words by Heart*. New York: Little, Brown, 1979.

Twain, Mark. *Pudd'nhead Wilson and Those Extraordinary Twins*. New York: Modern Library, 2002.

Volponi, Paul. *Black and White*. New York: Viking, 2005.

Wilson, Diane Lee. *Black Storm Comin'*. New York: Margaret K. McElderry, 2005.

Woodson, Jacqueline. *The Other Side*. New York: Putnam, 2001.

Nonfiction

Barney, William L. *The Civil War and Reconstruction*. New York: Oxford, 2002.

Beals, Melba Patillo. *Warriors Don't Cry*. New York: Archway, 1995.

Blumenthal, Karen. *Six Days in October: The Stock Market Crash of 1929*. New York: Atheneum, 2002.

Bolden, Tonya. *Cause: Reconstruction America, 1863–1877*. New York: Knopf, 2005.

———. *Tell All The Children Our Story: Memories and Mementos of Being Young and Black in America*. New York: Henry N. Abrams, 2001.

———. *Wake Up Our Souls: A Celebration of African American Artists*. New York: Harry N. Abrams, 2004.

Bridges, Ruby. *Through My Eyes*. New York: Scholastic, 1999.

Collier, Christopher, and James Lincoln Collier. *Reconstruction and the Rise of Jim Crow*. New York: Benchmark, 2000.

Crowe, Chris. *Getting Away with Murder: The True Story of the Emmett Till Case*. New York: Dial, 2003.

Damon, Duane. *Headin' for Better Times: The Arts of the Great Depression*. Minneapolis: Lerner, 2002.

Freedman, Russell. *The Voice That Challenged a Nation: Marian Anderson and the Struggle for Equal Rights*. New York: Clarion, 2004.

Greene, Meg. *Into the Land of Freedom: African Americans in Reconstruction*. New York: Lerner, 2004.

Hakim, Joy. *Reconstruction and Reform*. New York: Oxford, 1994.

Hamilton, Virginia. *Many Thousand Gone: African Americans from Slavery to Freedom*. New York: Alfred A. Knopf, 1993.

Hoose, Phillip. *We Were There, Too!: Young People in U.S. History*. New York: Melanie Kroupa, 2001.

King, David C. *Civil War and Reconstruction*. New York: Wiley, 2003.

Levine, Ellen. *Freedom's Children: Young Civil Rights Activists Tell Their Own Stories*. New York: Avon, 1993.

McKissack, Patricia, and Frederick McKissack. *The Civil Rights Movement in America: From 1865 to the Present*. New York: Children's Press, 1991.

———. *Days of Jubilee: The End of Slavery in the United States*. New York: Scholastic, 2003.

McWhorter, Diane. *A Dream of Freedom: The Civil Rights Movement from 1954 to 1968*. New York: Scholastic, 2004.

Rappaport, Doreen. *Free at Last! Stories and Songs of Emancipation*. New York: Candlewick, 2003.

Wormser, Richard. *The Rise and Fall of Jim Crow*. New York: St. Martin's, 2003.

Issues Related to Historical Fiction

Adamson, Lynda G. *American Historical Fiction: An Annotated Guide to Novels for Adults and Young Adults*. Phoenix: Oryx, 1999.

Brown, Joanne. "Historical Fiction or Fictionalized History? Problems for Writers of Historical Novels for Young Adults." *The ALAN Review* 26 (1) (Fall 1998): 7–11.

Brown, Joanne, and Nancy St. Clair. *The Distant Mirror: Reflections on Young Adult Historical Fiction*. Lanham, MD: Scarecrow, 2005.

Collier, Christopher. "Criteria for Historical Fiction." *School Library Journal* 28 (10) (August 1982): 32–33

Kaywell, Joan F. "Modernizing the Study of History Using Young Adult Literature." *English Journal* 87 (1) (January 1998): 102–7.

MacLeod, Anne Scott. "Writing Backward: Modern Models in Historical Fiction." *The Horn Book Magazine* 74 (1) (January/February 1998): 26–33.

Martin, Valerie. "Truth or Whoppers: On Writing Historical Fiction." *The Writer's Chronicle* 38 (4) (February 2006): 51–55.

"Teacher to Teacher: How Do You Incorporate History into the English Curriculum?" *English Journal* 89 (3) (January 2000): 26–30.

Paulson, Barbara A., ed. *The Historical Novel*. Washington, DC: Library of Congress, 1999.

Power, Chandra L. "Challenging the Pluralism of Our Past: Presentism and the Selective Tradition in Historical Fiction Written for Young People." *Research in the Teaching of English* 37 (4) (May 2003): 426–66.

Zarian, Beth Bartleson. *Around the World with Historical Fiction and Folktales: Highly Recommended and Award-Winning Books, Grades K–8*. Lanham, MD: Scarecrow, 2004.

Awards Received by Mildred D. Taylor

Career Recognition
1988 Children's Book Council Honors Program, "for a body of work that has examined significant social issues in outstanding books for young readers"

1997 ALAN Award

2003 NSK Neustadt Prize for Children's Literature

April 2, 2004, Governor of Mississippi Proclamation, "Mildred D. Taylor Day"

Individual Book Awards

Song of the Trees	Council on Interracial Books for Children Award
	Coretta Scott King Honor Book
	Jane Addams Honor Book
	National Book Award Honor Book
	New York Times Outstanding Book of the Year
Roll of Thunder, Hear My Cry	Newbery Award
	ALA Notable Book
	Notable Children's Trade Books in the Field of Social Studies
	American Book Award
	Boston Globe–Horn Book Award
	Horn Book Fanfare
Let the Circle Be Unbroken	Coretta Scott King Award
	American Book Award
	ALA Notable Book

	ALA Best Books for Young Adults
	Notable Children's Trade Books in the Field of Social Studies
The Friendship	Coretta Scott King Award
The Gold Cadillac	Christopher Award
Mississippi Bridge	Christopher Award
	New York Times Notable Book
Road to Memphis	Coretta Scott King Award
	ALA Notable Book
	ALA Best Books for Young Adults
	Notable Children's Trade Books in the Field of Social Studies
The Well	ALA Notable Book
	Parenting Reading Magic Awards Certificate of Excellence for Distinguished Achievement in Children's Literature
	ALA Quick Picks for Reluctant YA Readers
	Notable Children's Trade Books in the Field of Social Studies
	New York Public Library's 100 Titles for Reading and Sharing
	New York Public Library's Books for the Teen Age
	American Bookseller Pick of the Lists
	National Christian Schools Association Lamplighter Award
	IRA-CBC Teachers' Choices
The Land	Coretta Scott King Award
	Scott O'Dell Award for Historical Fiction
	Pen Center USA Literary Award for Children's Literature
	Los Angeles Times Book Prize Young Adult Fiction
	ALA Top 10 Best Books for Young Adults
	ALA Best Books for Young Adults
	ALA Notable Book
	Notable Social Studies Trade Book for Young People

ABC Children's Booksellers Choices Award
   Winner Young Adult Readers
Best Children's Books of the Year, Bank Street
   College of Education
Bulletin Blue Ribbons, Bulletin of the Center for
   Children's Books
Capitol Choices
Notable Children's Books in the Language Arts
Publishers Weekly Best Children's Books
Teachers' Choices, International Reading
   Association